THE FLOWERING PEACH

BY CLIFFORD ODETS

★

★

**DRAMATISTS
PLAY SERVICE
INC.**

© Copyright, 1954, by Clifford Odets
© Copyright, Renewed, 1982, by Walt Whitman Odets
and Nora Odets

CAUTION: Professionals and amateurs are hereby warned that THE FLOWERING PEACH is subject to a royalty. It is fully protected under the copyright laws of the United States of America, and of all countries covered by the International Copyright Union (including the Dominion of Canada and the rest of the British Commonwealth), and of all countries covered by the Pan-American Copyright Convention and the Universal Copyright Convention, and of all countries with which the United States has reciprocal copyright relations. All rights, including professional, amateur, motion picture, recitation, lecturing, public reading, radio broadcasting, television, and the rights of translation into foreign languages, are strictly reserved. Particular emphasis is laid upon the question of readings, permission for which must be secured from the author's agent in writing.

All inquiries concerning rights (other than amateur rights) should be addressed to Robert A. Freedman Dramatic Agency, Inc., 1501 Broadway, Suite 2310, New York, N.Y. 10036.

The amateur production rights in THE FLOWERING PEACH are controlled exclusively by the DRAMATISTS PLAY SERVICE, INC., 440 Park Avenue South, New York, N.Y. 10016. No amateur performance of the play may be given without obtaining in advance the written permission of the DRAMATISTS PLAY SERVICE, INC., and paying the requisite fee.

SOUND EFFECTS

An audio cassette containing the sound effects which may be used in connection with production of this play, can be obtained from Thomas J. Valentino, Inc., 151 West 46th Street, New York, N.Y. 10036.

> Sheep bleating
> Crickets & frogs
> Bird calls
> Rooster crowing
> Thunder

THE FLOWERING PEACH was first presented by Robert Whitehead, for the Producers Theatre, at the Belasco Theater, in New York City, on December 28, 1954. It was directed by the author; the scenery was by Mordecai Gorelik; the lighting by Feder; costumes were by Ballou; and the music by Alan Hovhaness. The cast was as follows:

NOAH	Menasha Skulnik
ESTHER	Berta Gersten
JAPHETH	Mario Alcalde
SHEM	Martin Ritt
HAM	Leon Janney
LEAH	Osna Palmer
RACHEL	Janice Rule
GOLDIE	Barbara Baxley
A STRANGE MAN	Sidney Armus
LION	Sidney Armus
FAWNS	Marjorie Barrett, Patricia Kay
GOAT	Barbara Kay
FIRST OLD MAN	Ludwig Roth
SECOND OLD MAN	Sidney Kay

THE FLOWERING PEACH

SCENE 1

TIME: *Then, not now.*
PLACE: *Noah's home.*

A simple living room is shown, a door on either side and two latticed windows in the back, the wooden furniture is almost primitive.
Dawn is near and a rooster crows far away as Noah enters slowly from the Right. Dazed, half in sleep, he moves to a table and drinks heavily from a water jug. Then he puts down the jug and sits slowly, thoughtful, puzzled—he is an old man, past seventy, at present bathed in perspiration, with a recollection of some horror, the pieces of which he is trying to put together in his mind. He starts abruptly, standing: The horror is complete!

NOAH. (*Enter* U. R.) No! (*Then, again.*) No, oh, no! (*He turns around the room, rolling and unsettled and, back at the table, dips a hand in the jug and runs his wet hand down his face and beard.*) No, please! . . . No . . . (*He puts his face in his hands and sobs with a bent head. Soon he has slipped to his knees and, elbows on a stool, is groaning and moaning with his head held between his hands. Esther, his wife, peers in from* R. *and asks after a moment:*)
ESTHER. Noah . . . ? (*Noah immediately gets to his feet, pretending nothing is wrong, although he cannot still his heavy breathing. Esther comes into the room—enter* U. R.) What'sa matter?
NOAH. Can't sleep . . .
ESTHER. Why, it's hot?
NOAH. (*Uneasily, annoyed. Crosses* L. *below table.*) I don't know. Go to bed, Esther—don't stand there! (*She follows him with her eyes as he moves away, saying mildly:*)

ESTHER. Hey, don't you get so fresh or I'll go over an' give you a slap in a minute. (*These sort of harmless remarks Noah has heard for so many years that he no longer has ears for them. He sighs.*)
NOAH. Maybe I'll take a drink.
ESTHER. (*Crosse C., sits bench R. of table.*) Don't take a drink. You drink too much.
NOAH. (*Belligerently.*) Who drinks too much?
ESTHER. (*Flatly.*) *You* drink too much. You think it's still a secret you drink too much? Why can't you sleep?
NOAH. (*Fiercely.*) Dreams! Dreams and more dreams! (*Then, pathetically.*) All I ask I should die in peace— (*Crosses R. to cupboard.*)
ESTHER. (*Calmly.*) You worked hard, now rest. Why should you die? We got three sons—
NOAH. (*Abruptly.*) Where is Japheth? Sleeping?
ESTHER. (*Annoyed.*) That's what you woke me up to ask me?
NOAH. I'll take a drink . . . (*He goes to a cupboard and pours a drink of arak or date brandy, drinks, puzzled, his wife watches.*)
ESTHER. (*Dryly.*) That's your breakfast?
NOAH. (*Defiantly.*) That's my breakfast!
ESTHER. (*Pausing, quietly.*) And what did you dream?
NOAH. (*Solemnly, taking a deep breath.*) Esther, tuchter, the whole world's gonna be destroyed!
ESTHER. (*Pausing.*) Our world? (*Noah nods in answer. A distant rooster crows again, the room is growing lighter. Esther is relieved that nothing is wrong with Noah except a foolish dream, however, she questions him further, with enjoyment and even a certain spite.*) And that was the dream? That's all . . . ?
NOAH. (*Nodding gravely.*) God appeared to me in a dream. (*Noah nods, looking at her with a heartbroken glance. She throws back her head and laughs loudly.*)
ESTHER. Noah, Noah, tell the truth—when they gave out the brains, you weren't hiding behind the house? (*Face austere and grim, he looks at her and goes to the closet for another drink despite her remarks.*) You had enough to drink. He pours and he pours, just like a pig.
NOAH. (*Loftily.*) You should be satisfied that I drink, otherwise I'd leave you. (*The drink in him, Noah wipes his mouth and sets himself a little grandly, head cocked to one side.*) Esther, hear me

what I say, Esther . . . God sent me a dream. Before him the earth is corrupt and filled with evil an' greed. You hear me? The end of all flesh is come. Everything that's living in the earth will be destroyed.
ESTHER. (*Jibingly.*) Thus spake the Lord?
NOAH. (*Warningly.*) You're not so smart, girlie! (*Crosses L.*)
ESTHER. (*Dryly.*) And how will all this happen? What, He'll make a fire?
NOAH. (*Crosses up to table. With inner seeing.*) A rain. He'll bring a flood—a flood of waters—so much rain the whole damn place will be drowned off! (*Sits bench L. of table. Turning away.*) I'm sick, I'm sick. My soul is sick! (*Watching him, Esther speaks with some uneasiness, for she is beginning to be worried by his condition.*)
ESTHER. (*Rises, crosses U. R.*) Why don't you come back to bed and get some sleep. I mean it—sleep all day—you won't be missed. (*Turns to him.*) By the way—who are you that God sends you a dream? Why, because your grandfather was Methuselah?
NOAH. (*Bristling.*) A damn good man, sister!
ESTHER. (*Jibing.*) Just like you and our three sons—damn good man!
NOAH. (*Unhappily.*) It's altogether too big a thing for me . . . (*Shaking his head, he sits wearily and pulls at his beard, and, beard and all, he looks like a lost little boy.*) I'm frightened. God give me too big an order here. (*Then musingly.*) Japheth should have children, get married. . . .
ESTHER. What're you sticking Japheth in the middle?
NOAH. (*Rises.*) Because everybody will go down in the flood, but we'll be saved—with our sons and their wives together. (*Crosses R.*)
ESTHER. (*Completely disgusted.*) Noah, I'm warning you—go back to bed or in a minute I'll tell you you're crazy! (*But Noah is looking upward, arms lifted humbly, sad, musing and devotional. Esther rails at him with a bitterness engendered by weariness.*) For a change do something useful around the house. Take a big stick—the house is fulla mice—kill some mice today. There's a few in the kitchen so fresh they stand there watching me cook. (*Noah sighs deeply, sniffs, wipes his nose with the back of his hand and starts for the cupboard again. Esther stops him sharply.*) And don't drink no more! You're sick . . .

NOAH. (*Flatly.*) I'm not sick!
ESTHER. So, if you're not sick, why should *we* be saved? And our sons with their wives, they're such bargains? Answer me a question, a *realism*—why should *we* be saved?
NOAH. (*Fiercely.*) This is not a "realism"! God's ready to destroy the whole world, so she wants a "realism"! (*Crosses* L.)
ESTHER. (*Rises. Relentlessly.*) You're lucky, you lunatic, I don't lock you up in the house!
NOAH. (*Bristling fantastically.*) Who'll lock who up in the house?!
ESTHER. You go in town with this story, they'll lock you up in a different house! *Your own sons'll lock you up!* (*Noah is about to make violent answer, but Japheth, his youngest son, enters* L.) And even Japheth here—your favorite son, he wouldn't hurt a fly—*he'll lock you up!* (*Crosses* R. *to cupboard.*)
JAPHETH. (*Mildly, half asleep.*) What's the matter here. . . ? (*Noah looks at him gloomily, he lays one cheek on the flat of his hand, a favorite mannerism. Smiling tolerantly, Japheth looks inquiringly at his mother.*) Drinking again. . .?
NOAH. (*Sharply.*) Never mind! These two hands—see them? —They still do a day's work! Where's Ham?
JAPHETH. (*Shrugging.*) Ham—Asleep in his own house, I guess . . .
NOAH. Shem? Shem's here?
ESTHER. (*Sits stool,* R. *Wearily.*) He's in Kadesh—
JAPHETH. Bringing in the olive crop. (*Kneels by Noah.*)
NOAH. Go get him. It's Friday today? Shem should be here tonight, before shabbos, before sundown.
ESTHER. (*Warningly.*) Shem won't like that, you know. He's maybe pressing already for oil and—
NOAH. Start soon, sonny, like a good boy, before it gets too hot.
JAPHETH. (*Looking to his mother. Rises.*) If that's what you want, I'll go . . . but what'll I tell him?
ESTHER. (*Indignantly.*) Shem and Leah won't leave in the middle of a crop!
JAPHETH. They'll ask me, Poppa . . .
NOAH. (*Thinking, abruptly. Rises.*) You'll tell Shem a big building proposition came up! The customer is very impatient, can't wait, understand? Needs an estimate right away, hear me?
JAPHETH. (*Puzzled.*) What, a house?

NOAH. (*Pertly. Sits L. of table.*) So much an' so much an' no more talk! (*Noah indicates that the conversation is over so far as he is concerned. Not wanting to make Noah seem foolish before a son, Esther waves Japheth out of the room, holds her smirking fire until they are alone again.*)
JAPHETH. All right!
ESTHER. (*Rises. Crosses to table.*) Now you did it good! First we had a flood—now we're building a house!
NOAH. (*Rises. With dainty cockiness and precision.*) Yes, old friend of mine, but not a house—an ark! A boat, three stories high—
ESTHER. (*Derisively.*) Yeh, yeh, yeh!
NOAH. (*Crosses D. L.*) Yeh, yeh, yeh! With doors and windows an' covered with a roof! (*Defiantly proud.*) And this ark, God says it, will float on the face of the deep!
ESTHER. (*Pityingly.*) An' that's what you'll tell our Shem when he gets here. He'll hit you with a stick!
NOAH. (*Crosses R. to stool.*) Eh, that ain't nice, girlie, that kinda talk . . . (*Weariness has returned to him and she watches him sit.*)
ESTHER. This time, I won't take your part against the boys—you'll sail alone, my sailor, on the lonely deep.
NOAH. (*Sits. Pensively.*) Lonely times is nothing new to me. . . .
ESTHER. You were a pest, that's why. Only *you* know God and His commandments—that's how you used to speak. An' the people they didn't like it. Maybe you'll stop talking and eat a pair of eggs?
NOAH. (*Annoyed.*) Don't wanna eat! (*She looks at him out of her staunch realism, but can't help admiring if whimsically his absolutism; besides, tired as she is, Esther is very fond of him.*)
ESTHER. Tell me . . . why don't I give you away for a good cat?
NOAH. (*With a lofty bite.*) This speaks for a loafer in the street, such a talk! Pfft! Go cook!
ESTHER. (*With a half smile.*) Yeh, today I'll start the shabbos bread early. It'll be hell when the boys get here. (*She starts across the room but swerves towards him, one hand lifted in mock slapping gesture. He backs away from her with a typical snarl, all part of an almost ritualized by-play between them.*)
NOAH. Keep away!

ESTHER. (*Coaxingly.*) Come here, I wanna feel your head.
NOAH. (*Crosses* U. R.) Keep away, hear me?! . . . (*Esther starts for the door again, murmuring, "Yeh, yeh, yeh, yeh," but stops and turns in the doorway.*)
ESTHER. Yeh, yeh, yeh, yeh. Tell me, fool, in your whole lifetime you ever even *seen* a boat?
NOAH. (*Turns to her. With huffy dignity.*) I seen a boat, many times—twiced!
ESTHER. (*Mockingly.*) Twiced. And where, by the way, are we when it rains?
NOAH. (*Crosses* D. *above stool* R.) Inside, floating around, decent an' dry, with all the animals.
ESTHER. (*Picking up her ears.*) What animals. . . ?
NOAH. (*Surprised at her reaction.*) All the animals—of every kind a pair, clean and unclean. Everything that creeps an' walks an' flies—
ESTHER. (*Incredulously.*) And all this God told you in one single dream. . . . ?
NOAH. (*Jaunting around. Crosses to table.*) Told it to me in one dream, yeh! (*Sits bench* R. *of table. As she nods.*) So now you know.
ESTHER. (*Sits bench* L. *of table. Slowly.*) Now I know . . .
NOAH. (*Unmoving, intently.*) Why am I so cold suddenly. . . ? Esther, you hear music. . . ?
ESTHER. (*Pausing.*) No . . .
NOAH. (*Lifting his hands simply.*) Lord. . . ? God. . . ?
ESTHER. (*Rises, slowly. A little frightened.*) Noah, stop it. . . . (*Noah slowly drops his hands and, without seeing or hearing her, permits his very concerned wife to seat him on a stool.*) Noah . . . you can't talk to God, Noah . . . That's a thing of the past. You're sick, Noah. You'll go in bed now and when Shem comes I'll—
NOAH. (*Snuffling.*) I'll be here when they come, right here. (*Not wanting to vex him further, Esther goes to the door, turning and looking at Noah: he is leaning a cheek on his open hand.*)
ESTHER. Call me if you want something . . . (*There is no answer and she goes,* L. *Alone, Noah rocks himself a little, as an old Jew does, in sorrowful musing, to comfort himself. When he speaks it is sole, humbly, sadly and with devotion.*)

NOAH. Lonely times again. . . .? (*Sighing.*) Now I must go out in the world an' make meself for a big nuisance again. . . ? (*Then.*) Why should she think I'm crazy? (*Abruptly standing.*) Now, just a minute! How do I know I'm not? I had a dream or not? (*Stamping his foot.*) Floor, listen to me! (*Slapping the table.*) Tell me, tell me, table—I had a dream or not? (*He listens, bewildered and fevered, but only silence answers him back, then he abruptly throws his arms upward and speaks angrily!*) If you spoke to me, Lord, I don't want it! I'm too old everybody should laugh in my face! I ain't got the gizzard for it—No, sir! (*Toning down to a softer devotional tone resting his mouth on clasped hands.*) Oh, God, excuse me— You are All and Everything an' I'm unworthy. You see me—what am I good for? All I do is cough an' spit. Pass me by—pass me by. Please. . . . (*Now the Presence of God is heard: it is expressed by a certain musical rustle or widening shimmer, as if a gigantic tuning fork had been struck, its vibrations stern and imperious. With this comes one long thunder roll [which in the theatre is made by one good union stage hand rolling a lead ball across the back of the stage.] Noah falls to his knees as if struck, his head is bowed low. After a moment he tilts his head a little and his nose twiches like a rabbit's. "Lord?" he asks. The musical shimmer deepens, spills everywhere and then softens.*) You came out, God. . . ? (*Then, listening reverently.*) Don't be mad. Because if I must, I must . . . I must? (*Sighing and shaking his head sadly. Gradually growing sly.*) What do I know about boats? Ast my Esther an' she'll tell you; when was I near water. Bread is bread, I know it— a pickle is a pickle, a knife is a knife—but boats? . . . (*Noah's slyness is reproved by a brief but angry thunder roll. Noah nods meekly but he is heartsick nevertheless.*) Awright, whatever you tell me to do, I'll do it. . . . (*Then nodding.*) Yes, I remember everything to a "T." The length of the ark should be three hundred cubits, fifty cubits the breadth an' thirty cubits the height. . . . (*Nodding again.*) I'll try to convince my sons to do what You say, but with my two oldest boys I'm altogether no good! You'll have to help me, 'cause they'll lock me up for a noisy old man. (*Abruptly.*) You're here yet . . . ? But wait a minute—the main point we didn't get to! You're talking a total destruction of the whole world an' this is something terrible—! (*He breaks off suddenly and gazes about, asking in a timid whisper:*) Lord. . . ? You're here. . . ?

(*He waits a moment and then painfully gets to his feet. The Presence of God has faded away into silence. Noah groans:*) Am I awake or am I asleep? I'm awake, but I wish I was dead. (*But, cocking an eye, he looks around him, wondering if he actually is awake or asleep. He leans his cheek on an open hand, and, whimpering a little, draws delicately into himself. Antiphonal roosters crow proudly in the distance. The stage lights dim out quietly.*)

CURTAIN

SCENE 2

TIME: *Later.*
PLACE: *The same room.*

Noah, austere and withdrawn, is sitting as before, one hand is up as if to shade his eyes, while listening covertly to the others. Realizing the basic foolishness of his position and claim, Noah means to keep both his temper and his tattered dignity if possible.
Outside the sun is a fiery ball about to sink and perhaps mitigate the impossible heat of the day. Esther is tired, muted and worried; it has been a very long day for her. She listens carefully and judicially to all that is said, in between stealing glances at Noah to watch his reactions and condition: if necessary she will come to his defense in a bustling way.
Japheth, the youngest son, listens silently while he carves a wooden spoon; were it not for an almost palpable intensity, he would be thought of as a modest youth in his early twenties: his mind is stubborn as it thinks and listens, as he feels and savors. The others because of a certain slowness and shyness in Japheth, have always thought of him as something half-wit and wayward, a most unjust view of this proud, private and thinking young man. Perhaps it is because Noah makes unconscious identification with Japheth that the boy has always panged the

old man's heart; they are two outcasts in the more competent and fluent world.

Ham, the middle son, is a neurotic, restless and highstrung man, frequently talking above himself in a loud biting voice; malice and jealousy are frequently masked in him as humor and good fellowship and sometimes even candor; he japes, jeers, derides and mocks, but he knows how to turn a politic phrase in the direction of his older brother, Shem, on whom his livelihood depends.

In the doorway stands Leah, Shem's smug and plump wife, she of the prim and small, disapproving mouth. She is a fit and sometimes prodding mate for her heavy and shrewd husband—Shem, the oldest son—sometimes shrewd to the point of foolishness; he looks like a weighty, worried boxer dog.

This, then, is Noah and his troupe, each of them awry and clownish in some way—assorted clowns and acrobats. Japheth—on stool D. L. Noah is seated D. R. in an armchair.

SHEM. (*Crosses* D. *around Noah and* U. R. *Enjoying his power.*) Poppa, I have to hear this again. I wanna get the points straight in my mind.

HAM. (*Above table. Impatiently.*) We've been over all the points —what's the use, Shem?

LEAH. (*Seated, bench* R. *of table.*) Someone should stop telling my husband what to do—he knows what to do.

ESTHER. (*At cupboard.*) We *heard* the dream four times awready, Sham. Whatta you bothering? (*With a wave of the hand she retires in disgust.*)

SHEM. (*Nettled but politely.*) I don't see what you're mad about, Momma.

ESTHER. My head's splitting awready!

LEAH. Don't be made at us—we didn't invite ourself here. We have eighteen olive pickers working up—

SHEM. That's six whole *shekels* a day and if nobody supervises them—

ESTHER. So why didn't you leave your dear wife there? We need her here? (*To Leah.*) Shabbos is comin'—it's getting dark. Go in the kitchen an' give a hand, instead of standing around like

a boss! (*The two women glare at each other, Shem tries to smooth out things, Ham smirks and snickers.*)
SHEM. Be that as it may, Momma—
ESTHER. (*Derisively.*) Be that as it may! Tell her to go in an' baste the meat! (*Shem, after a helpless moment, nods in an understanding way to Leah, only reluctantly does she go to the kitchen, Esther snorting after her, crosses to* L. *of table.*) She married the richest boy in the neighborhood, that's her trouble. (*Ham laughs and crosses* D. R. *of table and Shem turns his temper on him:*)
SHEM. Ham, will you stop it, willya? You're making me nervous with that laugh of yours! (*Then.*) What would you do if *you* were the *head* of the family?
HAM. (*Shrugging.*) I'm only the *middle* son.
SHEM. But you *work* for me, don't you, so let's hear what you think.
HAM. (*Abruptly.*) I'd lock him up—he's been *raving* for years!
ESTHER. Hey, don't you get so *fresh* or I'll—
SHEM. That's right, Ham. After all, *honor thy father and mother.*
HAM. How much honor did he give *me?* You can talk—you got everything he owns!
SHEM. That's the *law*, Ham. The oldest son—
HAM. (*Angrily.*) And the law says lock him up if he's nuts and *he is nuts!* (*Sits bench* R.) We all heard him, didn't we? No more world, but we'll all be saved! Why? Because we build a *boat?*
SHEM. (*Goggle-eyed with sobriety. Crosses* R. *to cupboard.*) Yep, that's what he said. . . .
HAM. Oh, I forgot to ask: When do we start, after supper or before? . . . (*Lapsing, Ham goes to the cupboard and takes a drink. Leah looks in, listening, spoon in hand.*)
ESTHER. Where's your wife?
HAM. Never mind my wife. (*Turning.*) You got a problem by the tail, Shem. What's this gonna do to your business name and prestige?
LEAH. Shem, he's right!
ESTHER. I'm ready to get in bed an' pull the covers up. . . . (*With a gesture of washing her hands of the entire matter, Esther starts out* L., *snatching the spoon out of Leah's hand.*) Japhie, watch the dirt! (*Exits* L.)
SHEM. (*Crosses* L., *sits bench* L. *of table. Turning.*) Now 'bout you, Japheth? What do you think?

HAM. (*Hooting.*) Oh, that one—he'll carve a few more wooden spoons for Momma, that's what he thinks!
NOAH. (*Seated armchair*—R.) Leave him talk!
HAM. Ah, the mummy's come back to life! (*Noah turns on Ham with a cold but contained fury:*)
NOAH. (*Rises.*) Why, you miserable no-good, you! What did you want me to leave you? Married to a fine respectable girl an' five nights a week he don't come home! (*Sits.*) What, to gamble away, you wanted? To spend on women? Pisst!
HAM. (*Smirking.*) Why discuss me? Isn't the fate of the world at stake?
JAPHETH. (*Seated, stool* L. *Quietly.*) You're part of the world . . .
HAM. (*Rises, crosses* D. C.—*sits stool. Mockingly.*) Make room there, Shem, the little one may say something big! (*Until now Japheth has scarcely lifted his head from his whittling. Ham's present treatment of his brother is a main reason that Japheth has become almost stammering mute, he becomes embarrassed or tense, wanting to either cry or fight. Ham has always been able to release his bottled-up wrath on his younger brother.*)
JAPHETH. . . . Doesn't matter.. . . (*Rises, crosses* R.)
HAM. (*With poised waiting.*) Kindly. . . ? Please. . . ?
SHEM. Stop it, Ham! (*Crosses* R., *follows Japheth.*) What about it, son?
JAPHETH. (*With slow unease.*) It hasn't r-rained since early Spring.
SHEM. Huh?
JAPHETH. F-f-floods are possible, I mean . . . (*Ham sniggers.*) If Poppa says he had the dream, he had it . . . he didn't make it up.
LEAH. Shem, it's getting late and if we're going back tonight—
SHEM. Just a minute, Leah. (*To Japheth.*) He didn't? (*Leah sits* L. *of table.*)
JAPHETH. No, imagining something so cruel as the end of the world isn't in Poppa's nature. (*Noah, with one listening ear cupped, is pleased. Shem, holding back the smirking Ham, is growing more confused and angry by the moment.*)
NOAH. Ah ha, you hear?
SHEM. He had the dream, he didn't— It's not in his nature— what the hell are you talking about?

JAPHETH. (*Stubbornly.*) I'm saying that Poppa's been sent a real vision.

NOAH. He understands.

SHEM. But do you understand the practical consequences if we took this serious?

JAPHETH. Of course I do. All life would be destroyed. . . .

SHEM. It would mean giving up everything I own to build a boat!

LEAH. And what about reaping and planting the autumn crops?

SHEM. Yeah, who'd do all that while we build the ark? The man in the moon?

HAM. (*Rises. Crosses* U. *to Shem.*) Shem, you're up in the moon yourself. If you build an ark, you believe in the flood. But, if you believe in the flood, why worry about crops?

LEAH. Exactly!

HAM. (*Enjoying it all.*) But if you *don't* believe in the flood, why build the ark? (*Sits bench* R. *of table.*)

SHEM. (*Turning on Japheth.*) You see where all this crazy talk is getting us?

HAM. (*Triumphantly.*) I told you not to start with him, Shem— he belongs out in the barn. (*Japheth slowly stands and, it would seem, makes a menacing feint in Ham's direction. But right at this moment Noah, who has drawn into himself, rocking himself in his chair, face on open hand, breaks into full and open lamentation.*)

NOAH. Oh, Lord above us, are we no more to see peace an' good in our day . . . ? This is a serious game . . . Give the people time to repent! Look in your pocket to forgive them . . . (*All his life Noah has broken out in prayer or song, no matter where or when, at will, as it suited his inner mood. His sons have stopped their bickering and are listening now, although Ham's face wears a broad smirk. Shem, however, has always been awed and made nervous by Noah in these moods. Esther enters briskly at this moment. Leah moves* L.)

ESTHER. You'll all stay for supper? —it's ready. (*Then.*) Oh, he's crying again? Like clock-work!

HAM. (*Brightly.*) Come on, Poppa—give it up as a bad job! (*Crosses* D. C.—*sits stool.*) Give us your blessing and Sabbath prayer. I'll stay for supper.

NOAH. (*Drying his tears.*) Don't do me no favors, sonny.

SHEM. (*Humoring him.*) All right, Poppa, don't get mad.

NOAH. (*Rises.*) God told you— He's speakin' to you in my

mouth—what you should do! (*To Shem.*) Bring in the harvest. Plenty of things needed for the trip—for forty days an' nights alone it will rain—
HAM. He's got us on that boat again!
NOAH. (*Right back at him.*) Lost my patience with you—an independent man's tellin' you! (*Turning to Shem, imperiously.*) A flood is coming. The world will be destroyed, but we'll be saved! And I don't say it again! (*Noah sits grandly. Shaking his head heavily, Shem is silently polling the room; Ham smirks at him. Tired and sort of sick at heart, Shem looks at his mother—she shrugs. Japheth's attention is no longer on his carving. Shem sighs heavily. Noah perks up his head when Shem approaches him.*)
SHEM. (*Above L. of him.*) Poppa, I'd like to say somethin' . . .
NOAH. (*Perkily.*) Yeh?
SHEM. Everybody in this room loves you; but nobody . . . thinks you're in your right mind. (*Ham steps in with the matter-of-fact air which usually covers his subtle disrespect.*)
HAM. (*Takes stool—sits L. of Noah.*) Yeah, did you ever give a thought to a simple item like the animals . . . ? You said, didn't you, a pair of each?
NOAH. (*Readily.*) Oh, some more than a pair. The clean ones, what you call kosher, *seven* pairs!
HAM. How do we capture just one pair? You know, something simple like lions or tigers . . . ? (*There is a pause as everyone looks at Noah as he begins to ponder the problem; thinking, he pulls his beard.*)
ESTHER. What'sa matter you're so quiet all of a sudden? Noo, tell him. Tell him how you'll go out with a big rope . . . (*And rattling off into laughter. Ham laughs—takes stool—crosses* U. R. C. *—sits.*)
NOAH. Hmmm . . . I don't know . . . (*Then.*) But wait a minute . . . God's not puttin' Himself up to be foolish! And if He says—
ESTHER. (*At table.*) Says, He says—*what* He says?!
NOAH. He would tell me a thing that it can't be done?
ESTHER. (*Making an end of it all.*) It's time to eat—everybody get washed! Leah, you'll stay for supper with Shem. Bring out the shabboth candles and clean off the table. (*Esther exits* D. L., *Leah, having received a nod from Shem, follows. The three sons are watching Noah, who has seated himself and is puzzling out the*

problem, muttering and gesticulating to himself with the quality of, "On the one hand, this, but on the other hand. . . ." etc. With Noah it is always like a moon sailing through broken clouds, in and out, here and not here. Now he has returned and, peering and craning his neck, he looks at Ham and Shem and rubs his chest, murmuring:)

NOAH. Tired. Hurts me, hurts me here. . . .

JAPHETH. (*Above Noah—a hand on his shoulder. Sympathetically.*) It's late, Poppa. I better go let the sheep in the fold.

NOAH. At least I got one son he believes me, a boy clean as rain. He'll go with me to the end of the way, won't you, sonny?

JAPHETH. (*Uneasily.*) Poppa, I see your dream . . . but it would be a bitter dose to take— (*Noah answers in his most lucid, and naive tone:*)

NOAH. Oh, yeh, it's bitter gall. So many poor people is bound to suffer. (*Then, firmly. Rises.*) No, if God gimme an honest dream, He'll prove it. (*Exits* U. R.)

HAM. (*Crosses* C. *Sits bench* R. *of table. Chortling.*) Fair enough! Can't ask for more, can we, Shem? (*Japheth crosses* L. *Obviously relieved by what seems his father's final attitude, Shem jovially slaps the departing Japheth on the back.*)

SHEM. Japheth . . . we don't spend as much time together as brothers should. But I take it that you're rather a thoughtful, dreamy type, right? And that's not to gainsay that you're mighty useful with your hands. Why don't you come work for me?

JAPHETH. What about Poppa's dream . . . ?

SHEM. I'll pay you well and you'd learn your way around. Listen, I'm a God-fearing man myself. What did Poppa have with all his piety? He gave away more than he kept—here's a little secret! Every man needs a model to get ahead . . .

JAPHETH. A model?

SHEM. So let's be friends, real brothers. . . . I'm offering you brotherhood. . . .

JAPHETH. No, you're not. You're offering me yourself as a model. Thanks . . . I'll think about it. . . . (*Crosses* R.—*Shem follows.*)

SHEM. What is there to think about, willya! Who are you? I suppose if God really ordered us to build an ark, you'd *think* about it!

JAPHETH. I'm thinking about it right now . . . (*Leah enters* L. *with spoons.*)
SHEM. I'm curious— You would or you wouldn't build the ark?
JAPHETH. Maybe I wouldn't . . . I might decide to die with the others. . . . (*Shem laughs.*) What's funny? Someone, it seems to me, would have to protest such an avenging, destructive God! (*Shem is aghast at such impious defiance, only Ham remains amused.*)
SHEM. Lemme get this straight! If the Supreme Being ordered—
HAM. (*Rises. Crosses to Shem.*) Wait a minute, Shem—we're up in the moon again! (*Ham crosses* U., *sits stool.*)
SHEM. I'll be honest for a change! Poppa's in his second childhood an' you're not outa your first! (*Noah enters* U. R. *with silver candlesticks which he puts on table—then sits in armchair.*)
NOAH. What is this? Brothers dasn't fight! (*Esther hurries in, putting a large sabbath bread on the table, Leah right behind her.*)
ESTHER. Honest, another fight? In a minute I'll pick up a broom an' one-two you'll all be out in the yard!
SHEM. (*Crosses to table. Pompously.*) I started talking to this boy, for his own good, about his future—
ESTHER. Everybody's hungry now—it's gettin' dark—we'll all sit down and eat!
SHEM. Look, supper's one thing, but this boy—
ESTHER. Leah, give me the spoons, bring the plates, I'll take the meat. When I think of what happened today I don't know what's real any more. We'll eat supper—that's real. (*She exits, preceded by Leah. Noah is beginning to wane into a ruminating, prayerful attitude in his chair. Shem, however, is still prickled with resentment and speaks balefully to Japheth.*)
SHEM. I'll have to teach you a few things about respect. He's gotta learn who's above him.
NOAH. (*Rocking a little with inner prayerfulness, mutters fretfully.*) Shabbos is comin' . . . quiet in the house . . . (*Japheth crosses to go outside.*)
SHEM. If Momma didn't like to have you around the house, I swear I'd get a court order and sell you into Egypt!
JAPHETH. (*Smiling thinly.*) I have to let the sheep in . . . (*Japheth exits* D. R. *Outside the sunset sky is aflame and colors the room. Shem speaks aside to Ham.*)

SHEM. That's one nut I'll crack if it takes all year. (*Esther enters with several dishes for the table.*)
ESTHER. Everything's ready. We'll eat. (*Leah enters—screaming.*) What'sa matter?
LEAH. There's a mouse, there's a mouse in the kitchen—he looked right at me!
ESTHER. (*Dryly.*) So look right back at him.
LEAH. (*Abruptly.*) Here it is—uh!
SHEM. Where? (*Leah points and jumps aside. This little flurry Shem and Ham preparing to catch the mouse, pulls Noah out of himself.*)

ESTHER. Get a stick an' kill it. I tell him every day—
HAM. There it is, a brown one! Head him off, Shem—he's gone your way!
SHEM. I'll step on him—pisst!
NOAH. A mouse?

} in unison

HAM. Watch it, Poppa—he's coming your way. (*Peering, Noah bends abruptly and apparently the mouse runs into his cupped hands; he heads off the approaching Ham.*)
NOAH. No, don't hit her—you dasn't, such a little thing.
SHEM. (*Sits bench R.*) What's the matter with you, Poppa—it's a dirty little mouse.
HAM. (*Crosses R. to cupboard.*) Squeeze his head and throw him out! (*Tenderly cupped in his hands, Noah lifts the mouse to his eyes; Esther jibes.*)
ESTHER. In a minute she gets a kiss, an old lady friend of his.
NOAH. (*Wonderingly.*) A mouse . . . ? No mouse . . . an olden time creature, a *gitka!*
SHEM. A what?
NOAH. (*Impressively.*) One was not seen even in my day . . .
HAM. A what, Poppa?
NOAH. Shh, gitka, shh . . . She breathes in my hand like a heart . . . (*Now a falsetto little voice is heard singing a wordless, sad and delicate song. Everyone stiffens or turns: What is that and where is it coming from!*)
HAM. Who's doing that?
ESTHER. What is it . . . ?
SHEM. It's— (*Noah is flushed with quiet excitement and tender pride.*)
NOAH. Esther . . . God has sent us a gitka . . . she sings for

us . . . (*There is an awed hush as the creature's wordless song continues. Meanwhile, sheep have been heard bleating without, now there are added to the sheeps' sounds a roar, a whine, a whinny and a soft insistent treadlike beat, all these sounds adding up to a kind of canonic music. Japheth enters quickly, repressing a strong excitement, calling, "Poppa!"*)

HAM. (*Intensely.*) Shhh!

JAPHETH. Momma . . . (*Japheth stops seeing the absorption of the others and hearing the falsetto song. Then the gitka stops singing, Shem steps back.*)

SHEM. That mouse is singing?

JAPHETH. Look out the windows, everyone! Poppa, look out the windows! (*Japheth doesn't move as Noah and Esther go to one window, while the others cluster at the second. A frozen silence, Noah mutters to himself, a moment later Shem tears himself away from the window and exclaims in a choking voice:*)

NOAH. (*Peering.*) More, Esther, is coming down the road?

ESTHER. Yeh, more . . . yeh . . . (*Leah has begun whimpering and moving away from the window. Dazed, leaning on a table, Shem is muttering, "No. No. No," etc. Ham's voice rises and hysterically.*)

HAM. They are standing beside the sheep!

SHEM. Don't want to see it!

HAM. Nothing is moving!

SHEM. Don't want to see that!

NOAH. (*Shading his eyes.*) Tuchter, what is by the fence?

ESTHER. Never seen such an animal like that . . . (*She turns and sits heavily on bench L. of table, Japheth takes her place at the window. A whirring of wings is added now to the animal sounds.*)

NOAH. (*Awed.*) Birds, too . . . ?

JAPHETH. (*Hushes.*) Some birds, yeh. (*Then.*) Those are gazelles watering in the yard. (*Shem kneels at bench—R.*)

LEAH. (*Abruptly in panic.*) Lock all the doors— (*Crosses to door U. R.*) We'll be killed!

HAM. (*Whirling around.*) She's right! We'll—! (*Crosses to D. R. —armchair—sit.*)

NOAH. (*Lifting his voice.*) Stand still where you are! Nobody should move! (*No one moves as Noah comes to the middle of the room, Shem is making a sobbing choking sound, as if he cannot catch his breath. Noah bends and lets the gitka run out of his hands, his eyes following its flight from the room. Everyone but Noah and Japheth, who have remained stunned at the window, have fallen to their knees.)*

SHEM. (*A mere babble.*) Oh, Lord, in Thy infinite wisdom, God, Thou hast seen fit . . . Thy power . . . I . . . I . . . I . . .

NOAH. (*With quiet power.*) Children, these are the creatures (and not all yet) who God has sent them . . . to enter the ark with us. They are sacred to us, and we are sacred to them. (*Then.*) Yeh, this was my dream. (*To Esther.*) Tuchter, get up—bring fire for the candles. (*Japheth is rigid and stunned, standing in the background. Esther goes to the kitchen and returns immediately with a lighted wood sliver.*)

HAM. (*Burbling.*) I always wanted to be a good man. Doesn't anyone believe me?

NOAH. (*Sternly.*) You could prove it. Go get your wife, Rachel, and bring her here . . .

HAM. (*Nervously.*) Through the animals? (*Noah nods, Ham hesitates for a moment, sniffs and then goes. Weeping and groaning, face in hands, Shem drags himself to his father's feet:*)

SHEM. Poppa, forgive me, forgive me! I didn't know . . .

NOAH. (*Gently.*) Be quiet, Shem. To me don't bow an' pray— you dasn't. Only to God above let us lift our voice with love and honor. (*Noah centrally placed behind the sabbath candles, the others group around him. Outside the daylight is sinking fast and with it the sounds of the animals. The men have covered their heads and Noah intones the traditional words over the candles as he lights each one, he blesses and lifts his head and his eyes are awash with tears.*) Japheth, come to the table. Oh, Lord, our God, the soul is rejoiced in Thee and Thy wonders. Here the family . . . is united to serve You as You asked. Give us strength and truth to serve Thee . . . (*The candles flicker a little. One of Noah's hands creeps to the corner of his mouth, as if to push back sobs. Outside a murmur of holy music is heard, mingled with the bleating of the puzzled sheep. And only Japheth, alone and horror-struck, stands outside of the tight family scene.*)

SLOW FADEOUT

SCENE 3

TIME: *Later.*
PLACE: *A high hillside cleared of trees, although two scrawny palms still stand between the raw stumps; these, the jagged stones and the parched grass patches give an arid and wild look to the scene. Only the stubby stern of the ark is seen at* R. *There is a hum of work in the air, the sounds of axes and hammer blows, of wood striking wood, and a few times an invisible workman calls, "Yo ho, yo ho," etc. etc.*

On view are three of the four women who one day soon will make the long trip by water. Esther, dominant as usual, is presiding over the wearying work of culling and packing into vats, crocks and baskets various fruits like olives, dates and figs. The women have been working for many weeks from dawn to dusk and they are tired. Rachel, Ham's wife, is her usual nervous and befuddled but bright and hopeful self; there is characteristically, about her an air of the delicate, the tentative and hesitant; she is seldom certain. Leah, differently than before, stubborn and smug, contentious and judgmental, her silences haughty and disapproving.

Above everything is the broiling sun. There is a spurt of wearied working rhythm, until Esther speaks, sharply.

ESTHER. (*Seated*—L. *end bench above table.*) Leah, watch out what you're doin'—don't let any bad fruit get in! (*Leah, seated* R. *end table—on stool—stiffens, mouth growing smaller, as Rachel says cheerfully:*)
RACHEL. (*Kneeling* L. *end table, sorting figs.*) It contaminates the good. . . .
ESTHER. Such damn heat I never seen it in my life time! We'll stop soon and eat. Tastier dates we never put away.
RACHEL. Try the figs, Momma, they're delicious.
ESTHER. (*Regretfully.*) Figs you need teeth for . . . (*Taking another date.*) Here's a nice big date that says, "Eat me, eat me!" Awright, don't be in such a hurry, I'll eat you. I see the boys comin'. They must be thirsty. Go Leah, bring water, a fresh bucket. Rachael, you'll take cows' milk. (*She thrashes the air*

around her as she sits fanning herself with a branch of green leaves.) Mosquitoes something terrible. . . .
RACHEL. I'm surprised they come up this high.
ESTHER. Leah, what're you carryin' that big buncha keys? What'sa matter you're so swell all of a sudden? (*Leah answers with a proud look and with her bucket exits, following Ham, disgruntled but wearied, who has passed from* L. *to* R., *carrying a long, half-peeled log. Esther laughs.*) Leah, I never liked too much —stubborn you know. An' nothin's good enough for her. Her mother, the old lady, the same way. (*Turning.*) How long, Rachel, are you married to our Ham?
RACHEL. Five years . . . why? (*Rachael smiles politely and vacantly: as now, she frequently is "not here," for direct personal contacts make her nervous. Esther is looking right at her and nodding thoughtfully.*)
ESTHER. It's a long time to be unhappy. Maybe I could teach you a few things on the trip. Go, take the milk. . . . (*Rachel smiles nervously and goes, Esther watching her.*)
RACHEL. I have a lot to learn.
ESTHER. (*Nodding.*) But you're a fine person.
RACHEL. Thank you, Momma . . . (*Grateful for a kind word, Rachel exits awkwardly* D. R. *Esther sighs, fanning herself and cocking a calculating eye at the sky. She turns when she hears sounds at* L.)
ESTHER. Is that you Noah . . . ?
NOAH. (*Unseen.*) Yeh . . . (*Enters* U. L. *More tired and older than ever, looking backwards at the animal park off* L. *He is carrying several cucumbers which he hands to Esther.*) Who ever seen such a thing . . . hundreds of animals to stand without a sound. I'm worried for the teeger [tiger]. Japhie fixed his foot yet?
ESTHER. Dunno . . .
NOAH. (*Crosses to table.*) A few fresh cucumbers, nice size. No new animals came today? (*Esther shakes her head, Noah looks up in a tree ahead.*) It's beautiful, the (h) eagles . . . the king of birds. Look, they're lookin' at me . . . Polly wantsa cracker . . . ? (*He wiggles two fingers in the birds' direction and sits painfully.*)
ESTHER. You'll take a bite?
NOAH. I lost me appetite to eat . . . (*In a bitter flash.*) **I can't**

do a man's work an' it hurts me! (*Lapsing.*) No, my dear lady, I'm no more the man who invented the hoe an' the rake . . . (*Connected, but both disconnected, they sigh.*)

ESTHER. You know, I'm really surprised more *people* don't come around.

NOAH. (*Crosses u. c., picks up gitka cage.*) Loafers, you mean? Trouble makers? The ark is old news awready. (*Hawking and spitting.*) I miss meself a little drink now an' then. I'm worried for the gitka, too. Who knows today where to find her a mate . . . ?

ESTHER. (*Rises.*) Worry better for our Japhie. Where'll he find a mate. (*Temper and strength appear immediately in Noah; he sits up alertly, shaking his head.*)

NOAH. (*Puts gitka down. Crosses D. to her.*) Esther, Japhie don't act right nowadays—too fresh. I thought for sure he'll go, a fine decent boy, in the great footsteps of his fathers. But whatever I say—like talkin' to a wall—

ESTHER. That's foolish.

NOAH. (*Bristling.*) Not to give proper respect is foolish?

ESTHER. He's tired. Whatta you want? Almost by himself he's building the whole ark!

NOAH. I do give him credit, but we don't fit to each other if he don't give respect. Disrespect to a father is disrespect to God!

ESTHER. (*Firm but mild.*) He's *your* son—tell him to take a wife.

NOAH. (*Haughtily sad. Crosses L. to bench.*) Such a boy, so strange, what could he offer a decent girl? (*Sits.*)

ESTHER. (*Promptly.*) He could offer her a nice boat ride! (*She enjoys the remark with her rattling laughter and shoos away flies with her leafy fan. Noah has put his face on an open hand, musingly, and doesn't see Japheth come in from U. R. This son is no longer a boy, it is plain to see; there is a responsible and mature air about him, but he is also very tired, distracted and even a little dazed, he is "marching to the sound of another drum," it would seem. While he is drinking from the spring Esther calls to him.*) We'll eat in a few minutes, Japhie.

JAPHETH. (*Turning.*) What, Momma?

ESTHER. We'll eat in a few minutes.

JAPHETH. Fine, I'll just put a poultice on the tiger's foot. (*Starts out L.*)

NOAH. And how is the teeger's foot today . . . ? (*Unhearing, Japheth continues on his way to the animal park, wiping the perspiration from his face. His mother's voice stops him.*)
ESTHER. (*Sits.*) Japhie, Poppa's talkin' to you . . .
JAPHETH. (*Crosses* D. R. *of Noah.*) Oh, excuse me, Poppa, I was thinking about ten things at once.
NOAH. (*Coldly.*) I ast you only one thing—how is the teeger's foot?
JAPHETH. I'm putting a poultice on the tiger's foot right now. (*Starts out* U. L.)
NOAH. (*Correcting him.*) Teeger, nicht tiger! (*Japheth is rather puzzled by his father's attitude, but he doesn't mean to quarrel with him.*)
JAPHETH. (*Pleasantly.*) Fine, Poppa, you say teeger and I'll say tiger. (*Crosses* D. L. *of Noah. Hesitantly.*) And while it's on my mind, Poppa . . . what about a rudder for the ark?
NOAH. (*Frigidly.*) You mentioned it before, no? Well, don't mention it again. The good Lord steers the ark, not us—
JAPHETH. Excuse me, Poppa . . . that doesn't seem right.
NOAH. (*Angrily.*) You see, Esther. Everything's a damn fight with him!
ESTHER. (*Waving Japheth out* U. L. *After a moment, flushing, the son goes, it of course being true that a subtle resistance to Noah and the ark project has built up in him. Esther rises. Stolidly.*) You're fighting! . . . I wouldn't lie, you're in a very crabby mood today!
NOAH. (*Rises.*) In my day a father had to tell a son twenty times to go and take a wife . . . ? (*Esther, grown exasperated, fixes Noah with a baleful eye: Her patience may slip in a moment.*)
ESTHER. A better son than Japheth you don't have. (*Scornfully.*) And instead of having such a big mouth, capting [captain], maybe you should tell him we can't get along without him.
NOAH. What, I'll lie to him?
ESTHER. Lie? Try for a week to build the ark without him! You big fool, you! That's how you talk to a boy his body is one sweatin' blister?
NOAH. (*Pacing. Loftily.*) Just like you an' me, he sleeps at night.
ESTHER. Sleeps? You hear God! So why don't you hear a boy cry every night?

NOAH. (*Turning.*) He cries . . . ?
ESTHER. Every night! To God, God an' God again! God should make him a good man! He should spare the world, the children. . . . (*She turns away, and wipes her eyes. Noah is stopped, sorely puzzled, hurt, tenderized, but he asks, finally, with shrewd probing:*)
NOAH. (*Crosses to her.*) Now, just a minute there, old friend of mine . . . to which God is he cryin' . . . ? You see out there over the mountains? Fifty an' sixty gods they got.
ESTHER. (*Sornfully.*) So who tells you our God is best?
NOAH. (*Abruptly passionate.*) Because, dammit, girlie, He's the One who does all the work! He knocks them, all the other ones, their heads together, don't He? (*Crosses L. Sits bench. Esther wants to say more but goes to the table and tosses some food around, for Shem comes in from D. R.*)
SHEM. Ready to eat?
ESTHER. Ready to eat . . .
SHEM. (*Calling off R.*) Ready to eat! (*He goes to wash, U. C.—then crosses D. R.—sits stool R. of table. Leah enters D. R., sits above table R. end. Rachel enters D. R., crosses to spring U. C. Ham enters D. R., crosses to spring. Esther pours water from a pitcher over Noah's hands and he daintly rubs his fingers together, his face has grown sad and tender and he speaks in a wistful murmur:*)
NOAH. Hmmm . . . he don't sleep, poor boy? I do give him honor, a good boy. . . .
ESTHER. (*Crosses to Noah.*) Wash your hands and take a bite.
NOAH. You told me the truth, Esther?
ESTHER. (*Stolidly.*) Only the truth. (*Ham stops to watch Rachel, she has gone closer to the animal park and is calling out, with a sense of some wrong:*)
RACHEL. Japheth . . . ? Japheth, food's ready. . . . (*When she returns to the table Ham is standing right there, watching her sardonically.*)
HAM. How beautiful are thy feet with shoes, oh prince's daughter. Get me a plate of food in a hurry, Sam . . . (*She hurries to the task. Ham crosses U. C. to spring, washes hands—then sits rock U. R. C. Japheth comes in, takes some food and sits at L., alone, there is evidently much unfocused hostility between him and his*

older brothers. *Noah steals a few glances at him. Esther sits on rock* U. C., *tired and not eating. Shem, beside his wife, picks up one of the fresh cucumbers.*)

SHEM. Say, fresh cucumbers—it's early. You brought them, Poppa?

NOAH. Yeh, plenty more next week.

SHEM. (*Pleased.*) It's the Kazan seed—it's an early grower, without rain. Leah, make a note—remember! (*Takes knife and peels cucumber. Leah merely nods, being an automatic memo pad for anything which suggests possible gain.*)

RACHEL. (*Takes plate to Ham.*) Momma, can I give you something?

ESTHER. I'll wait. (*Rachel sits above table—*L. *end.*)

NOAH. (*To Shem.*) Next week I'll go in town for wheat an' barley seed. We need what, about twenty quarts each?

SHEM. Yeah, but they won't sell it, Poppa, and I know whereof I speak.

JAPHETH. When I was down in town last week they—

SHEM. (*Sharply.*) Just a minute, son, I'll tell him! (*Shem glowers at Japheth. Esther doesn't miss the byplay.*) What they claim in town is that since we think they're so wicked—

ESTHER. (*Rises.*) The story happened to Japhie, didn't it? So why do you shut him up?

SHEM. Who shut him up? (*Ham rises, crosses to table for food.*)

ESTHER. You an' Ham always shut him up!

HAM. (*Lightly. Starts back* U. R.) Well, children should be seen and not heard. (*Japheth throws his bread at Ham—then turns and abruptly walks out* L.)

SHEM. (*Rises, crosses* U. R.) I won't lie, Momma—if that boy comes near me again I'll gore him like a bull!

HAM. Success has gone to his head!

SHEM. (*Pacing up and down* R.) No doubt about it—he's very skilled—but he's no boss over me!

ESTHER. (*Quietly.*) Who is boss over you?

SHEM. Who? Poppa, God—

ESTHER. Who's building the ark every day, stitch by stitch, Poppa, God? (*Leah rises.*) You sit down, Leah! (*Leah sits.*)

NOAH. (*Murmuring.*) Fair, a fair question.

SHEM. (*Crosses to her. Confused.*) Be that as it may, Momma—

ESTHER. What can you build, coins one on top of another? (*Shem sits stool—*R. *of table. To Ham.*) And you, what? A pile of empty bottles in a back yard? (*Pausing, she looks at Noah. Noah nods his head sagely, saying crisply:*)

NOAH. (*Rises. Crosses to table. Esther sits bench* L.) In this regard Mother is a shrewd an' respectable one hundred percent right! (*Japheth enters* U. L.)

HAM. (*Statement.*) What about the rudder . . . ? He tries to boss you, too!

SHEM. Yeah, that's right—!

JAPHETH. (*Crosses* D. C. *to Noah.*) It's NOT right! I never bossed anyone in my life! (*Shem crosses* U. R.) But Shem and Ham have bullied me for years, and what they don't like, Poppa, is that I won't stay bullied! I admit it—I may be excitable from time to time, but I love you, Poppa, and I always will. You're the only master in my life—you taught me everything I know. I respect and revere you like you were dead.

NOAH. (*Dryly.*) Thanks . . . (*Pausing, doubtful of the compliment.*) But you're changed, Japheth, in different ways, too.

JAPHETH. Because I insist upon a rudder? I can't help it—a rudder is vital to the health of the Ark. Would you want me to lie?

ESTHER. (*To Noah.*) You want him to lie?

NOAH. (*Hushing her.*) I'm here, ain't I . . . ? (*Then, to Japheth.*) Sonny, the Supreme Being who selected us—He made me the Chairman, didn't He? He'll see I don't fall outa the chair! (*Then.*) But I asted you, for an instance, maybe five times to take a wife. . . .

JAPHETH. (*Pausing and squirming.*) But how can I do that, Poppa? How can I take a wife in times like these?

NOAH. (*With gentle insistance.*) But God tells you to do it, don't He? The new world will need babies, bushels an' bushels of babies.

JAPHETH. And what about the bushels of babies who will die in the flood? Since you bring it up . . . is this vengeful God the very God I was taught to love?

NOAH. (*Recoiling.*) Sonny, you mustn't, you dasn't talk this way . . .

JAPHETH. Forgive me, Poppa, but I must! Because I can't stay here!

NOAH. (*Turning cold.*) Can't stay here . . . ?
JAPHETH. No, I can't! I cannot work for this brutal God!
NOAH. (*Slowly.*) The Lord is good for anybody an' everybody, at all times! He was wonderful for the world in the old days an', blessed be His name, He will be for the new days to come! . . . (*With a real grandeur Noah has said the last word and turns away. Crosses* U. R. C.)
JAPHETH. (*Removes apron—tosses on bench* L.) If you won't forgive me, you'll have to forget me . . . you and Momma . . .
SHEM. (*Crosses to him. Incredulously.*) You mean you're walking off this job! (*Rachel rises.*)
JAPHETH. I won't be back . . . (*Exits* D. R.)
SHEM. (*Enraged.*) That boy's hands should be chopped off! (*Agonized, on the verge of sobbing, Japheth starts out* D. L. *Noah has brought his clasped hands to his mouth and is rocking faintly, in prayer. In Rachel's and Esther's eyes there are tears. Rachel sits.*)
ESTHER. His hands should never hurt . . .

CURTAIN

SCENE 4

TIME: *Later.*
PLACE: *As the last scene.*
Work has come to a virtual standstill. The weather is as before, the foliage dustier, everyone listless, irritable and drowsy.
Only Noah and, of course, Japheth, are absent. Esther is fanning herself, seated L. *end of bench above table. Shem is pacing anxiously—looking off* L. *Leah is seated* R. *of table peeling potatoes. Ham is stretched out comfortably on a higher hillock, asleep. Rachel is finishing a fine piece of sewing, sitting on ground* L. *of table.—A crude ramp runs* U. R. *to the ark.*

SHEM. (U. L. *Crosses* R. *to bench between Leah and Esther.*) What time did you say Poppa left this morning?

ESTHER. Was still dark. He went to town for seed. (*Shem crosses* U. C.)

LEAH. (*Primly.*) I hope he didn't go look for that blasphemous boy.

SHEM. (*Crosses* D. *to Leah. Reproving.*) Leah! Where's your brains? Who'll do God's work without that blasphemous boy? (*Rachel rises—crosses* L. *Sits bench.*)

LEAH. But Shem is the expert on seed. . . .

ESTHER. Maybe Poppa feels useless. Maybe he went to town for seed to be a big man. You begrudge him a little self-respect? (*Esther fans herself quietly and answers Leah without looking.*)

LEAH. (*Rises.*) Is this enough potatoes?

ESTHER. Enough potatoes. . . . (*Leah starts out* R. *with her starchy burden, but to turn and see Noah arriving from* L. *It is a little man, not a big man, who is returning, he is discouraged, tired and sweaty, with a staff in one hand, he eases two slung bags off his shoulders and stops to catch his breath. Rachel immediately brings him a cup of water which he takes and drinks. Ham awakens—sits on rock* U. R. C. *Shem crosses to Noah's* R. *Rachel rises, crosses* U. C., *gets cup of water, hands it to Noah, then crosses* D. L. *Sits stool.*)

NOAH. (*Sits rock* U. C.) The road is baking . . . I'll sit a minute. . . . (*He sits and, breathing heavily, looks around, drinks finally asking:*) Anything new . . . ?

ESTHER. (*Knows that this is a question concerning Japheth's where abouts.*) No. Nothing came. Nobody . . .

NOAH. (*Pausing.*) Somebody watered the animals in such a heat?

SHEM. Yeah. . . .

NOAH. (*Rises. Crosses* D. L. *Hawks and spits cotton before saying:*) Startin' tomorrow. Shem an' Ham, you'll continue the building work. The hanimals I'll take care of meself. We can't afford it to wait. Time is gettin' tight. (*Sits bench* L.)

HAM. What's in the bags, Poppa? (*This humiliating subject Noah is less ready to talk about, he wipes his mouth and answers reluctantly.*)

NOAH. Good wheat seed . . . not enough. Had the money but couldn't git myself more.

LEAH. (*Implying judgment.*) Why not . . . ?

NOAH. Wouldn't sell it to me, that's why not! (*Leah exits* D. R.

The violence of Noah's reply blows Leah out of the scene, potatoes and all. Noah stands, shaking his fist at the valley below.)
ESTHER. *(Rises.)* What happened?
NOAH. No, I'll start to cry . . . it'll hurt me . . . *(Rises. Then:)* They stoned me outa town! *(Crosses to table. All are aroused and aghast. All rise.)*
SHEM. Stoned . . . ?!
ESTHER. You had a fight? You're hurt?
NOAH. *(Shem crosses D. L. below bench. Esther sits stool R. of table. Very peppery.)* I went into his yard, this what's his name? —Ard, son of Hesh! "Oh, what're you looking for here, Poppy?" "Seeds, seeds an' seeds again!" *(Ham crosses D. C.—kneels—then sits.)* "But you look tired," he says. "Maybe you'll take a drink?" *(Primly.)* "I will not, no thank you," I says. "It's me new habit. I come just to buy seed," I says. "So help me God before a holiday!" *(Incredulously.)* An' he begins to laugh, hear me? An' he tells the crowd, "Ha ha, ha ha! Here's that lying old rummy Jew, Noah, that old two-doubles an'-a-chaser man! Now he claims the world is comin' to an end!" I'm gettin' madder an' madder— everywhere people is pushin'—and this Ard, I says to him: "Don't gimme none of your backtalks, because I knew you for a little bit of a baby," I says. "Don't open your mouth like your father, 'cause I'm here an' he's not!" I says. "And your father," I says, "when he *looked* good he didn't look good!" . . . *(He stops a moment, breathing thin fire, finally dropping his voice to a sort of hoarse, strangled whisper. Esther is clucking sympathetically, following the story intently.)* Next thing you know I'm rollin' over an' over in the dust of the road. . . .
ESTHER. In the road . . .
NOAH. An' then the stones! Hundreds! I couldn't count 'em even! Looked to me half the town was there: "Don't come back, you old faker you, with the flood and the ark and your crazy sons together!" *(Shem by now is on his feet, doing as he orders:)*
SHEM. Get a stick, Ham! Let's go!
NOAH. No, what'll it help?
SHEM. *(Grimly.)* I might get some peace of mind out of it!
NOAH. You'll fight half the town? *(Noah has quietly fallen back into his sad, musing attitude. Esther is looking him over, feeling his body, but he pulls away.)*
ESTHER. Where does it hurt?

NOAH. (*Solo.*) But one thing . . . my pride comes back to me . . . I'm no more ashamed for the crowd. . . . (*Looking at the eagles.*) But such a skinny thing of a body, what could you do? If God would only gimme a hinch what's his idea. . . . (*Japheth enters from* D. R., *father and son look at each other, for a full moment before Noah breaks the silence by snuffling and turning away; actually he longs, sorrowfully, to embrace Japheth, with relief and love, but outwardly he remains rejecting. Even Esther cannot interfere in this awful moment, to her eyes Japheth looks frightful, for he is bruised, unwashed and unkempt. Noah rises, crosses* D. L. *to bench.*)

JAPHETH. Poppa . . . (*Noah, back turned, shakes his head violently, that is all.*) Poppa . . . give me . . . your b-blessings . . . (*He steps in and falls at his father's feet, bowed, his face in his hands.*)

NOAH. (*Talking to a tree top.*) For what shall I bless you, for what . . . ? All the good looks of your soul is gone . . . you are a black mark!

SHEM. (*A little awed.*) But if he says to you, Poppa, that he's sorry—

NOAH. (*Fiercely.*) It's no more for a little person like me! It's between him an' The Almighty now!

ESTHER. (*Crosses saying:*) Get up, Japhie. Go wash yourself, boy, you're a mess. (*Crosses* R. *above table. But Japheth, it seems, is not finished, for more than contrition is written on his face:*)

JAPHETH. (*Rises.*) The ark can't be built without me. For your sake, Momma, and Poppa's, that's why I came back—for the family, not for God.

NOAH. (*Vexed beyond endurance.*) A story like this, big as Adam—*bigger* maybe—*such* a story you put yourself against?! (*Noah sits bench* L.)

SHEM. Be reasonable, Japheth. In the face of catastrophe like this, a man bows his head, shuts his mouth an' does his work! Right now you got Poppa so twisted—

JAPHETH. Talk only for yourself, Shem! And never again talk for me! You, too, Ham—I warn you b-both! (*Crosses* R. *below table—sits stool* R.)

ESTHER. (*Abruptly.*) Shem, go see—someone is on the ark. (*Shem whirls around, his first impulse being to pick up a stick. Crosses* U. C.)

SHEM. (*Calling.*) Hey, what're you doing up there?
HAM. It's a girl!
GIRL'S VOICE. Looking around . . . and around and around . . . (*Enters ramp* U. R.)
ESTHER. Who's this . . . ?
JAPHETH. She came from town with me . . . (*Noah, Esther and Rachel turn and look at him, he drops his eyes, embarrassed. By this time this girl has appeared, smiling and looking around with a very natural ease and curiosity. She thinks of these people as freaks, but with real interest and not with superiority. This, plus a chatty, informal, easy-going and humorous quality, makes her attractive on sight.*)
GIRL. (*Crosses* C.) Frankly, I didn't believe it. I mean everybody knows the story by now, but who'd think you'd take it serious enough to build that boat! Oh, this must be Noah. . . .
JAPHETH. (*Rises. Uneasily.*) Goldie, this is my mother . . . and my father. . . . (*Just at this moment Noah hawks and spits, apologizing immediately.*)
NOAH. Excuse me, I didn't spit for you . . . I just spit. . . . (*Japheth sits. Headed by Esther, the atmosphere is not friendly and Goldie senses it now, dribbling off with:*)
GOLDIE. And this is the other two brothers . . . ? (*Shem crosses* U. R. *Frowns, but Ham smiles—Goldie may be a stranger to the world of his parents, but she is no stranger to his!*)
ESTHER. (*Suspiciously.*) What is it, Japhie? You met Miss Goldie somewhere . . . ?
JAPHETH. She saved my life last night. (*Noah is immediately impressed, Esther reacts by a certain stolid intentness, for she has had immediate reservations about Goldie.*)
GOLDIE. (*Laughing.*) And don't think he's exaggerating! People hold grudges, you know, and they're superstitious—they don't like this flood business.
ESTHER. (*Quietly.*) An' what about you?
GOLDIE. The flood? Well, tell me, can you give it a real thought?
LEAH. (*With hauteur.*) And what did you come here for?
GOLDIE. (*Naturally.*) To take a look and go home, that's all. (*Of Japheth.*) They tried to set fire to him last night!
NOAH. (*Shocked.*) Fire . . . ?
GOLDIE. They were drunk, of course.
NOAH. Poor men . . . their name is not human.

GOLDIE. (*Confidently.*) No, they're very human, that type—like moody monkeys. I know human nature. After all, it's natural. You tell me I'm no good. Well, I know I'm no good. So what can I do, like you . . . ? (*Ham chuckles with appreciation, Noah speaks out of a musing sadness.*)
NOAH. But many, I heard, are goin' now more regular to synagogue. . . .
GOLDIE. They're just killing time. And time is killing them. Yes, something's in the air nowadays . . . people are troubled, not happy . . .
ESTHER. An' what about you?
GOLDIE. (*Crosses* D. R. *below table. Shrugging.*) Why be personal? But I'll say one thing. When was a poor person ever happy? Or a motherless child . . . ? (*Man enters* U. L.)
ESTHER. (*Stolidly.*) Which are you?
GOLDIE. Both . . . (*She stands behind Japheth* D. R. *She smiles beautifully and in this moment Esther, not giving up her serious reservations, half likes her.*)
HAM. (*Rises, crosses* U. R. C.—*to Shem.*) Who's he? Do you know? (*Shem shrugs. He is a man who looks like a shrewd, bored butler, and as if he belongs there, he walks squarely to the center of the scene wiping his hot face. Goes to table, picks up some figs. Noah rises, crosses* U. L.)
MAN. What're you located up so high for? It's a bad walk in this sun.
RACHEL. (*Rises, crosses* U. *to spring.*) I'll bring you some water. . . .
MAN. (*Crosses* L. *to bench, sits.*) Thanks, that's more'n my wife'll do. Who's Noah?
NOAH. (*Crosses* D. R. *of him. Shem crosses* D. R. *of Noah.*) That's me, Noah, son of Lamech.
MAN. Who's Shem?
NOAH. He's Shem.
MAN. You got a big bunch of animals out there. What for?
SHEM. They're grazing—
MAN. All the rumors I heard. So save your breath.
NOAH. Whatsoever rumors you heard, it's the truth. (*The Man sighs, bored, eyes Noah cynically, and, accepting the water, says thanks.*)

SHEM. (*Alertly.*) Tell him nothing, Poppa. (*To the Man.*) Whatta you want here?
MAN. I'm a deputy from the treasury department—taxes. (*Noah is puzzled. Rachel brings him a cup of water—then sits stool L.*)
NOAH. What does he want? . . .
SHEM. (*Crosses U. R. C. Looking at Leah.*) Taxes, so he says. But I don't know on what.
MAN. You know on what.
LEAH. (*Crosses D. L. end of table.*) You mean on the animals?
NOAH. The animals are the creatures of God.
MAN. God gave them to you as a gift? Well, that's taxable, too. Now, look, you good and foolish folk, I can forget the animals—they're not really covered by section four. But so far as other matters are concerned—
SHEM. (*Turns to him. Flatly.*) We own no assets, real or otherwise!
MAN. —I need a declaration and a fat down payment. Now, what about it? It's beginning to bore me—it's just a low grade living with me.
HAM. (*Crosses D. R. of Shem. From nowhere.*) Shem, I thought you were going downhill to pick cucumbers. . . .
SHEM. What????
HAM. (*Crosses to Man. Blandly.*) There's some very nice juicy melons in that field, too . . . (*The Man turns quietly and looks, other looks are exchanged. For the life of him Noah can't make out what is happening. Japheth has seated himself but is listening with averted face.*)
MAN. (*Admitting something.*) I happen to be fond of juicy melons. (*Ham crosses U. R.*)
SHEM. (*In the act at last!*) Yeah, these are beauties! You going back to town?
MAN. In that general direction, yah. . . .
NOAH. (*Crosses D. between Shem and Man.*) What is this . . . juicy melons? What's goin' on?
JAPHETH. This man came to collect taxes, and Shem is about to bribe him.
MAN. That's a very serious charge you make, young man!
ESTHER. (*To the Man.*) Do me a favor, Mister, an' shut up, yeh? (*To Shem.*) Shem, what did you sell? (*Ham crosses up ramp.*)
SHEM. Nothing! (*Crosses U. L.*)

ESTHER. (*To Man.*) You, what do you want here?

MAN. (*Angrily now.*) Taxes! Taxes on the sales of almost thirty thousand shekels worth of land and orchards! (*Noah turns and looks reproachfully at Shem and he tries to brazen it out.*)

SHEM. It's in his imagination—he can't prove a thing!

NOAH. Shem, I'll warn you not to twist me head around! Take the money, all the money, an' give it to him!

SHEM. (*Crosses to Noah. Blinking.*) Give it to who?

LEAH. (*Crosses to Noah. Quickly.*) Who says there's any money to give?

NOAH. (*Bitterly.*) On the ark nothing will be for sale, no investments, hear me? Money is unholy dirt on the ark—

SHEM. But when the ark lands and our children—

NOAH. Give it away! And don't answer a father back!

SHEM. (*Despairingly.*) I'm not, Poppa, *but what am I without my money?!*

ESTHER. (*Suddenly.*) Leah, give me those keys around your neck . . . (*Leah answers by clutching the keys and looking with dismay at Shem; he tries to covertly shake his head. Esther simply steps forward, jerks the chain off Leah's neck and hands the keys to Noah.*)

NOAH. (*Thinly.*) From where are these keys . . . ? (*Crosses D. to table—sits.*)

LEAH. Nothing, I wear them like beads— (R. *of him.*)

JAPHETH. The big one is from the stone summer cellar at Kadesh.

NOAH. Ah! . . .

ESTHER. (*Jibingly.*) Like beads . . . (*Sits* R. *of Noah. Shem's face is deliberately blank but dangerous. Noah, sick at heart, says to the man:*)

NOAH. Come here, sonny, I'm too tired to move. (*Man crosses* R. *to Noah.*) You'll go to Kadesh an' find an old cedar door, with iron hinges— (*Shem snatches the keys from his father's hands just as Noah is about to hand them to the Man. Shem stands at bay, murderous.*)

SHEM. Everything I am is in this key! I don't give that up easy! (*Leah moves up behind Shem.*)

JAPHETH. (*Rises. Abruptly.*) Give Poppa the keys . . . (*Shem turns on his younger brother with hate:*)

SHEM. You I'll tear you apart with my naked hands! (*Japheth's*

answer is to take off his shirt. Noah steps to him, saying, "I don't want fights! No fights!")
JAPHETH. (*Crosses* U. C.) You've got fights . . . (*Esther gently pulls Noah back. Now the two brothers face each other.*) Poppa wants the keys. He is mandated by Jehovah and he wants the keys . . .
NOAH. (*Trembling.*) Esther, they mustn't fight, mustn't. . .
SHEM. (*Pushes Leah away—she crosses* U. C.) Stop him, Ham—
JAPHETH. Don't move, Ham . . . (*But Ham, of course, has no intention of moving. Japheth advances into Shem, saying, as the later steps backwards:*) The keys, p-please . . . (*Shem's sudden answer is to throw a blow at him; Japheth steps back and avoids it, but Shem follows with others, the keys in one hand giving terrible striking power.*)
NOAH. He'll kill him with the keys!
ESTHER. Let them . . . (*Which is what Shem is doing in the trading of blows; then he stumbles and Japheth gallantly lets him get up, this enrages Shem so that he goes completely wild and in this time Japheth connects heavily with his head and knocks him out. Breathing heavily Japheth takes the keys out of Shem's hand, and crossing, gives them to his father who accepts them wordlessly; the old man's face is a study as he looks at the keys and the prostrated Shem. He beckons to Man who crosses to him —stepping over Shem's prostrate body.*)
NOAH. Go to Kadesh . . . I told you before. . . .
MAN. (*Accepting the keys.*) You got strong convictions. I admire the insanity of your belief! Good luck! (*Crosses* D. L. *and exits. Leah is at Shem's side and Ham has brought her water. Shem is groaning and trying to get up.*)
NOAH. (*Rises.*) What, he's saying something?
RACHEL. (*With nervous solemnity.*) He says, "Get a receipt." (*Heartsick, with mingled feelings, Noah crosses* D. L., *sits bench —musing with his face laid on a hand. Japheth has seated himself at the spring; he, too, finds mingled feelings within.*)
SHEM. (*Lumbering to his feet—helped by Leah.*) Some days it's better to stay in bed. (*He starts* R. *for the ark, Leah anxiously behind him. For a moment it seems that he will stamp a foot out at the seated Japheth, but he exits heavily* U. R. *with Leah behind.*)
NOAH. He'll tell me next, he was saving the money for a rainy

day. (*Esther's eyes travel between Noah and Japheth and the others. She is thinking. Rachel exits* D. R.)
GOLDIE. Well, I guess I'll start back to town. (*Crosses* U. C. *Ham crosses* D. *to her.*)
ESTHER. Take a bite before you go.
GOLDIE. I will—I'm feeling a little empty. (*She crosses* D. *to the table and helps herself to some figs which she nibbles thoughtfully. Esther crosses* U. C. *to Japheth. Ham follows* L. *of her.*) I feel depressed. You people really believe this, don't you?
HAM. Uh huh— Did I ever see you in a pageant?
GOLDIE. Might be. . . .
HAM. (*Crosses* U. C.) Would you like to see the animals?
GOLDIE. Where are they?
HAM. Only out there—thirty, forty yards. (*They exit* U. L.)
ESTHER. (*Quietly.*) So, you grew up, my son . . . (*Her son wants to show no feelings but abruptly he turns his face down to the ground and his back is shaking with sobs.*) Long life to your face, my dear . . . (*She moves across now to Noah,* D. L., *sorrowful, aloof and unhearing. Rachel takes an armful of odds and ends out to the ark.*) Noah, you'll take a bite now? Noah? (*Crosses* R. *above table to* R. *end.*)
NOAH. ("*Returning.*") Heh . . . ? (*Then.*) I'm beginnin' to wonder to meself—why did God pick this family. With none of my sons I don't fit. (*Crosses to* L. *end table. Sighing.*) Japheth's got a wife?
ESTHER. (*Warningly.*) Later.
NOAH. She's a nice girl? (*Japheth rises, takes bucket from spring, exit* U. L.)
ESTHER. Later. . . . (*He stands with his sense of grieving shame, his eyes caught by the eagles in the trees.*)
NOAH. (*Crosse* D. C.) Nobody's so good as God can be . . . but it's up to Him to gimme what I need to do His work . . . (*Holding out his hands.*) See them bones? That ain't hands no more, it's bones! (*Looking upward.*) You say to the eagle, fly! Even to a little bitty of an eagle like me, fly, fly higher an' higher! But You have shrinked away his wings and he couldn't do it! Why did You pick me . . . ? Honorable Sir . . . ? For what? (*A pastoral pipe plays in the distance. He stands, forlorn, comic and deeply touching, tears in his eyes, his sincerity blind and utter, his communication with God immediate and direct. Esther is moved and*

remains silent until Noah with a deep sigh, returns to her.) **Esther,** I'm tired to death . . .

ESTHER. *(Crosses to him—below table.)* Lay down a while.

NOAH. *(Nodding.)* I miss meself a little drink now and then. . . .

ESTHER. *(Guiding him* U. L.*)* Here in the shade, behind the bushes. . . . *(She helps him to a frizzy bush, he lies down heavily, sighing and saying:)*

NOAH. I'm worried, Esther, for the gitka . . . *(Esther watches him as he rolls and mutters, finding a comfortable position, and, being an innocent man, Noah is asleep in a moment. Esther looks at him and turns back to pick up her leafy fan, then she looks up at the hot sky with a sad heavy face, for she senses all of the agonies ahead. Crosses* R.*, sits bench above table. Meanwhile, Japheth, recovered, has quietly filled two water buckets and taken them out to the animal park. Now the delicate and tactful Rachel returns. Enter ramp, crosses to above Esther.)*

RACHEL. *(Lovingly.)* Can I do anything for you?

ESTHER. Shh, my husband's asleep . . . I'm washed out like a rag. . . . *(Then.)* How do you like that girl?

RACHEL. *(Lamely.)* I . . . don't know what to make of her. . . .

ESTHER. A person like her, she fits to Ham. *(Solemnly.)* The way you fit to Japhie. . . . *(Then.)* Rachel, I'll tell you your trouble in a nutshell—you got a habit of mind that nobody loves you. A fine girl like you, a good housekeeper an' everything!

RACHEL. *(Pausing, softly.)* Are you making fun of me, Momma?

ESTHER. Why?

RACHEL. You . . . say I'm a good housekeeper, but I'm the worst one in the district.

ESTHER. Because you don't have confidence. You think no one believes in you.

RACHEL. *(Shyly.)* Do you . . . believe in me?

ESTHER. *(Promptly.)* Of course! *(Rachel crosses to look* L. *Nods, being too moved to speak. Ham and Goldie return, laughing, in good spirits, except that she is preoccupied.)* Shh . . . Poppa's asleep . . . *(Ham crosses to spring* U. C. *Goldie,* C.*)*

GOLDIE. Well, I saw the animals. The tiger's the only one that frightened me.

RACHEL. *(Politely.)* Not the lion?

GOLDIE. The lion? Why, he's a real lamb—cute! *(Ham grins and, picking up a pair of buckets, returns to the animal park.)*

Your son, Ham, is an amusing boy—quick witted. (*Crosses* D. C. *to bench above table. Uncomfortably.*) What're you looking at?
ESTHER. You saved my son's life—I have to thank you.
GOLDIE. Don't mention it. . . . (*Crosses* R. *above table.*)
ESTHER. (*Turning.*) A wind . . . ? Where's a wind all of a sudden? (*Crosses* L. *below table. To above* L. *of table. Out somewhere a bird has begun to sing a throbbing song. Both girls turn, listening, but hear nothing. The vibrant humming presence of God has begun to shimmer broadly over the scene; in the background Noah twitches and mutters in his sleep, later crying out several times, as if in pain. Esther is amused.*)
GOLDIE. (*Pacing nervously.*) I don't think I'll be able to get back to town before dark now . . .
ESTHER. So don't stand on ceremony an' stay over night.
GOLDIE. (*Nervously.*) You keep looking at me. . . .
ESTHER. (*Stolidly.*) Maybe I like you.
GOLDIE. And maybe you don't. Why am I so nervous? Listen, tell me the truth, why did your husband give the man all that money? Why does this family have all those animals?
ESTHER. (*Quietly.*) Why? Because the world is comin' to an end. . . . (*Goldie looks at both the women, incredulity and a sense of the ridiculous fighting a growing conviction that something uncanny is in the air. She starts to giggle but it strangles off.*)
GOLDIE. (*Sits bench above table.*) Frankly . . . I feel faint . . . have to sit . . . must be the heat. . . . (*She sits, shaking her head in a dizzy way; then she abruptly puts her face in her hands, sudden weakness and panic mounting in her.*)
ESTHER. (*Pouring from jug—hands her a cup.*) Take some water. (*Abruptly there are frightening sounds and a thrashing around from behind Noah's bush; Esther looks at Rachel, turns, calls, "Noah?" and hurries to her husband; the sounds grow even more violent.*) Noah? What'sa matter, Noah? (*What she sees must frighten her, for she calls to Rachel, who obeys her immediately.*) Rachel—get the boys! (*Rachel runs to ramp calling Shem. Turning.*) Noah! Noah, wake up! (*Having bent down to wake him, she suddenly stands up and, strangely alarmed, bellows for her sons:* "Japheth! Shem, Shem! . . ." *Everyone comes running. Shem enters ramp. Japheth enters* U. L. *Ham follows. Goldie sits awry, in a half-fainting condition.*) Poppa's sick—wake up Noah! Hold him down, he'll hurt himself! (*Japheth and Shem take hold*

of their thrashing father, only his legs protruding from behind the bushes.)
JAPHETH. Poppa, what's the matter? Hold his arms, Shem.
SHEM. Poppa, wake up!
NOAH. (*Heavily.*) Ehh! Ahh! Uhh uhh! (*Abruptly Shem drops his father's arm and stands back, frightened, now Japheth does likewise albeit in slow motion, whispering, "Poppa . . . ?" More of Noah shows, on all fours, he seems to be coming out of an epileptic trance, all the others draw back, but Esther stands her ground, ready to help if only she knew how. But even Esther steps backwards when Noah gets to his feet, for he has become a young man of fifty: his eyes are eagle-bright, his reddish hair shows only one streak of grey and his beard is smaller but glowingly alive! The Presence of God fades away. Goldie rises. They all back away. Ham* L., *Japheth* D. L., *others* R. *Esther is the first one to find a faltering voice: "Noah . . . ?" He feels sick and blinks, grunting, "Heh? Heh . . . ?" Esther steps toward him, he shakes his head as if drunk.*) Esther . . . tuchter . . . what? . . . I took some drinks . . . ? (*Waveringly.*) Look, they're lookin' at me . . . what, I'm drunk . . . ? (*He sees his firmly-fleshed hands, he starts and feels one hand with the other, then, while his hands quickly explore other parts of his body, he squints narrowly at Esther. Falteringly.*) Esther— (*Slowly.*) God gave me . . . strength . . .
SHEM. (*Sotto voce.*) I'll go off my head in a minute. . . .
NOAH. We thank You, oh, Lord, for every kindness which You give . . . (*Noah abruptly freezes, sniffing like a dog. He is near Goldie and she shrinks back, horrified and fascinated by what she has seen.*) Something's burning?
HAM. (*Sniffing.*) No, sir, you smell the cedar grove.
NOAH. (*Chuckling.*) A wonder! I'll smell my favorite smells again—grass—lemons! (*He tears up a handful of grass and inhales its odor hungrily as he strides to the table and picks up a lemon, squeezing it to a pulp. This brings him face to face with Goldie. She runs to Rachel at ramp.*) Don't be afraid for me, girlie. I won't hurt you.
GOLDIE. (*Awed.*) I saw this with my own eyes . . .
NOAH. (*Turning, crossing* C.) Japheth, you got yourself a wife—a decent, respectable girl, she looks to be. (*Sealing it.*) She saved your life—you owe her, don't you . . . ? (*Japheth makes no answer and Noah moves in to his sons, speaking briskly. Crosses*

U. S. C.) Boys, keep clear. Between us there should be no more fights. (*Crosses* D. L. *To Japheth.*) How long more for the ark to be finished? For an instance . . . ?
JAPHETH. Nine to eleven weeks.
NOAH. And if I work, like on roofin'?
JAPHETH. Less. (*They all watch Noah as, nodding and thinking, he bends to pick up his staff from bench* L. *Japheth is very tense, for he has never seen this Noah before. Without thought, Esther realizes that all the little bridges between her and Noah are broken. One thing is obvious to all: Noah has become the strong head of the family again.*)
NOAH. Esther, gimme a few figs in my pocket, yeh? (*Crosses* C. L. *of table. In a friendly way.*) I'll forget, Japheth, all your foolish remarks. But be careful for the future. Because Somebody Upstairs, He hears you, every word. So you'll build the ark, but maybe you won't sail on it. (*Esther crosses* L. *to bench with figs wrapped in napkin.*)
JAPHETH. I don't intend to sail on it. (*Noah's eyes flick from Esther to Shem and back to Japheth before his grip tightens on his staff and he steps in closer, Japheth standing his ground. It is Esther who steps in between them, giving Noah the figs.*)
ESTHER. You ast for figs. . . . (*Noah puts the packet in his pocket but his eyes stay on his son's face. He hawks and spits before saying to Esther:*)
NOAH. I'll be back late tonight or tomorrow.
ESTHER. Where you gone?
NOAH. (*Crosses* U. C.) In town . . . for seeds! . . . (*He looks in Japheth's face again, grips his staff firmly and walks out* U. L. *with proud strength. No one moves.*)

FADEOUT

CURTAIN

SCENE 5

TIME: *Later.*
PLACE: *The same place as before.*
More of the ark is seen, as if it had slipped down its slope

a little. Everything has begun to wear a disordered, helter-skelter look. Prominent is a loom on which the women have been weaving a woolen cloth.

Not only is the dimming and swelling afternoon light frightening by its very instability, but a terrorizing solar manifestation exists; for the second day now the swollen sun, blood red at both its terminals, has clearly reversed itself and even now is riding across the hectic skies from west to east!

Back and forth, like a file of ants, the women of the party are carrying various foodstuffs and household articles to the ark. More than once, stopping to rest or wipe away the sweat, they will glance covertly at the awesome skies. Esther is tired but seems calm and clear. Leah is irritable and troubled, but a feeling of importance gives her an air of determination and authority. Rachel is treading as if on eggs, but, somehow, she wears a prim and orderly look. It is Goldie who is most liable to go to pieces; she is worried and even suffering from severe shock.

Later the heavy silence will be broken by a few working noises. But just now only the droning of a cicada and the song of an invisible bird are heard. Noah and Shem, standing, are looking far down the valley; it is a long moment before Noah speaks. Leah crosses L. to R. with a bag of grain. Rachel chosses L. to R. with bowl.

NOAH. (*Looking out front standing* C.) . . . So what do you think . . . ?
SHEM. (L. *of Noah. Awed.*) I think you're right. I never seen clouds that size. . . .
NOAH. (*Anxiously.*) You think I'm right? Any day, now?
SHEM. Any hour. If there's a wind, any hour.
NOAH. You hear, Esther? Any hour, he thinks, if a wind comes.
ESTHER. (*Seated bench* L.—*sewing a piece of wool. Stolidly.*) Yeh. It's lucky we took the animals on board awready. (*Esther looks up at the sky. There is a moment of brooding silence, fringed by the distant bird song. Only Esther sees Japheth enter* L. *with his "luggage" which he puts down on bench* L. *before looking out at the valley for a moment.*)

SHEM. (*Incredulously.*) The sun rising in the west and setting in the east! Why don't the people see? Where are their brains?
ESTHER. (*Quietly.*) So what should they do if they see . . . ?
NOAH. (*Still peering.*) Pray!
JAPHETH. For what? . . . (*Noah and Shem turn and look at Japheth, but he turns and without another word walks out L. In the background Ham, watering the animals, comes and goes with a pair of buckets.*)
SHEM. (*Crosses U. C.*) That attitude—it's gonna cost him dear, that attitude. (*Enter Leah, Rachel—R. Cross L.*)
ESTHER. And it's gonna cost us dear, that attitude.
SHEM. I'll take this stuff up, Momma. (*Take roll of matting, exit R. to ark. Ham follows from spring with buckets.*)
ESTHER. 'll be nice. You're tired, girls. Sit a minute. It won't run away.
LEAH. We'd rather get it all on board, Momma. (*Calling back to ark.*) Goldie! (*Girls exit U. L.*)
NOAH. (*At table.*) I never expected in my lifetime that Japheth's ways should be bad ways. . . .
ESTHER. I keep thinking of old lady Kamen. A grandmother nineteen times! What'll happen to her? (*Goldie crosses R. to L.*)
NOAH. An' what'll happen, old friend, to thousands and thousands of others? (*Crosses to her.*) Woolen cloth you made? What for? (*Leah and Rachel cross L. to R. with loads.*)
ESTHER. Old people get chilly, you forget. . . .
NOAH. You're lookin' at me? Why?
ESTHER. Just lookin'. (*She has picked up a large, wide hat decorated with fruits, berries and flowers. Actually she is flirting with him. Goldie crosses L. to R.*) I found it last week. Maybe from thirty years back. (*Puts hat on.*) I'm pretty? You'll take me for a walk?
NOAH. One thing, sister—with such a hat you couldn't go hungry.
ESTHER. (*Takes off hat.*) It's good for sun. I'll take it with.
NOAH. Esther, I'm worried! The ark is finished and the ark is ready. Japheth is serious? He won't go . . . ?
ESTHER. (*Shaking her head.*) He won't go.
NOAH. But he took a wife . . . ?
ESTHER. He didn't "took." You gave him a present.
NOAH. (*Correcting her.*) God gave him!

ESTHER. (*Mutely.*) Let it be God. . . .

NOAH. Tell me, he'll stay behind, you think? Our Japheth is such a dummy-man?

ESTHER. (*Insistently.*) Talk to him nice. Don't yell at him—persuade him!

NOAH. (*Angrily.*) Look at the sky! With what should I persuade him? (*Crosses* R. *below table.*) He's off his head! (*Girls enter. Leah crosses* L. *for cloth. Rachel crosses* L. *to Esther.*)

ESTHER. So treat him like he's sick. Because I'll swear to you one thing, Noah—if he don't go, I won't go! (*Goldie sits bench above table.*)

NOAH. (*Balefully.*) You're crazy, too, old friend of mine! (*He walks away, agitated and troubled. Exits* D. R.)

RACHEL. (*Crosses to Esther.*) Why don't you rest, Momma? I can finish this.

ESTHER. (*Muted, refusing.*) Got a funny habit . . . I gotta keep my hands busy. . . . (*But suddenly she puts her hands to her old face, Rachel, standing behind her, holds her tightly with understanding.*)

LEAH. (L. *of bench—picking up cloth.*) We'll get all this woolen cloth on board. Every time I turn around, Goldie, you're sitting down. (*Rachel exits* U. L. *Returns—crosses* R. *with load—exits* R.) There's work to do!

GOLDIE. I'm staying here.

LEAH. Why?

GOLDIE. I can't get up . . . (*Leah haughtily walks out with the cloth, Rachel following with more of same. Goldie sits miserably, Esther tries to put her at her ease.*)

ESTHER. You're nervous, tuchter?

GOLDIE. (*Appreciatively.*) You called *me* daughter . . . ? Doesn't this make *you* nervous?

ESTHER. (*Grimly.*) The last few weeks, like everyone else, I'm in the bushes five time an hour! (*She stands abruptly and goes to the table.*) How do you like it? My husband forgot to eat. (*Ham enters* R.—*crosses to spring with buckets.*)

GOLDIE. (*Hesitantly.*) Would you do me a favor? Tell me . . . not to be nervous.

ESTHER. (*Gently.*) Awright, I'll tell you . . . don't be nervous . . . (*Pats Goldie, puts hat on bench above table—walks out to the ark—exits* D. R. *as Ham puts his buckets at the spring, seeing*

Goldie is alone he approaches her, his manner rather furtive. Goldie is startled but doesn't turn when he speaks.)
HAM. (*Crosses D. above her.*) Hello, snake. I'll see you tonight.
GOLDIE. No you won't. I won't meet you again.
HAM. What're you so scared about? Nobody knows.
GOLDIE. (*Unturned.*) I don't want anything to do with you. I was frightened and gave in to you.
HAM. (*Sarcastically.*) With your background, you frighten very easy. What was it, hysterics? (*Touches her shoulder.*)
GOLDIE. (*Standing. Crosses L. to bench.*) It was hysterics and I'm on the verge of hysterics right now, so go away!
HAM. (*Moves toward her. Firmly.*) Don't raise your voice! I'll see you tonight.
GOLDIE. (*Back U.*) No, I'd rather go and tell your mother the truth—you blackmailed me! (*She moves to a basket and lifts it.*) I'm warning you, Ham. I'm not very stable. If you don't go away I'll begin to scream—! (*With Ham watching her nervously, she holds onto herself and, breathing deeply, walks out to the ark just as Rachel returns. Ham starts for the spring but Rachel returns . . . she stops him. Goldie exits R. Rachel crosses L.*)
RACHEL. (*On ramp.*) Ham, how can you be so gross? She's near hysterics—let her alone.
HAM. What do you mean, "let her alone"?
RACHEL. Your mother knows, but don't let your father find out.
HAM. (*Eyeing her tauntingly.*) Are you jealous? . . . .
RACHEL. (*Coolly.*) Be careful of your father . . .
HAM. (*Smirking.*) The circle is complete. I married you because I thought it would get me in good with my father! (*Grinning, he exits L. Proud and hurt, Rachel doesn't move. Esther returns, R. ramp, glancing at Ham's receding back.*)
ESTHER. Up and down it's worse than stairs. (*Rachel turns away with a shake of the head. Sighing. Esther sits and, lips pursed, looks ahead stolidly.*) He's a black stone, but I thought he'd make a good husband.
RACHEL. (*Unhappily.*) What makes a good husband . . . ?
ESTHER. (*Picks up hat from bench.*) Noah was a good husband.
RACHEL. Was? He's still very much alive, Momma.
ESTHER. Yes . . . and I'm an old woman. (*Puts hat on table. Then, stolidly.*) Japhie woulda made a good husband . . . now he'll make a better corpse . . .

RACHEL. (*Distressed.*) He hasn't changed his mind? (*Crosses to Esther.*)
ESTHER. (*Heavily.*) No . . . (*Sits bench above table, then.*) Rachel, I'll ast you the truth. You love him, don't you . . . ? It's only between you an' me an' my old hat.
RACHEL. Yes.
ESTHER. Now, listen tuchter—I don't show it that's my habit, but I'm old and very tired. I charge you to help me now. Speak to him, before it's too late.
RACHEL. What would he do for *me* that he won't do for *you*?
ESTHER. (*Tapping her head.*) I don't know, but . . . make him feel he's wanted . . .
RACHEL. (*With swift sincerity.*) Momma, I'll try . . . (*Seeing Japheth, enter from U. L. with another piece of luggage, Esther abruptly covers the subject on hand by saying.*)
ESTHER. The hat is nice, heh? (*Rachel glances around quickly and picks up the first object she touches, saying:*)
RACHEL. Excuse me, I'll take this on board and be back. (*Takes basket L. end table. Exits up ramp.*)
ESTHER. An' your bedding, don't forget . . . (*Japheth puts down the baggage and looks off at Rachel as he advances with silent feeling across to his mother, standing behind her and holding her arms tightly.*)
JAPHETH. Momma . . .
ESTHER. (*Stolidly.*) What's that, more baggage? You're in such a hurry?
JAPHETH. (*Crosses R. above her.*) You're mad at me, Momma?
ESTHER. I can't be glad at you, sonny. Suddenly you're a stranger—nobody knows you. Why is that? (*Enter Old Man D. L.*)
JAPHETH. Sometimes that happens when a boy grows up.
ESTHER. And to what did you grow up? To die in the cold cold water? (*She looks past her son at an Old Man who has entered from D. L., two of his companions, as old as he, lingering behind. Japheth sits R. of her.*) You want to drink, Mister? Help yourself.
OLD MAN. Thank you. God is good . . . (*Crosses U. C.*)
(*Esther emptily replies as her eyes shift back to her son.*)
ESTHER. I'm really surprised nobody came here today, except these olden time religious. (*Dropping her voice.*) Poppa expects you'll marry that girl. He won't take her without you . . . you like her?

JAPHETH. She's a perfect stranger to me.
ESTHER. Ham likes her very much . . . a tested recipe by now . . . and Rachel knows it.
JAPHETH. (*Quietly, looking at his hands.*) Momma, do me a last favor . . . tell Poppa the ark needs a rudder . . .
ESTHER. (*Angrily, standing.*) He don't care about that now! He's worried about *you*, the way I am, the way Rachel is!
JAPHETH. (*Rises.*) Momma, don't be mad at me . . . love me, always love me . . . (*He tries to embrace her but she stands away, holding him off, crosses D. C.*)
ESTHER. Go away from me! How can I love you now?
JAPHETH. (*Follows her.*) Those are terrible words, Momma—!
ESTHER. You just got rich, that's your trouble—you just became a man an' you're spending it as fast as you can, throwing it in everyone's face . . . remember what I say! (*The Old Man goes with a filled water pail, murmuring again, while intermittent bird song nearby.*)
OLD MAN. God is good. (*Crosses D. L. and exits.*)
ESTHER. (*Emptily, with a curl of her hand.*) God is good. . . . (*She exits D. R. below the ark. Japheth doesn't see her but already Rachel is standing on the ramp, ready to approach him. He starts L. and picks up a piece of his baggage, his eyes are caught by the valley below and he straightens up and looks out earnestly. Rachel approaches him from behind. Crosses D. R. of table.*)
RACHEL. What do you see out there in the valley, Japheth?
JAPHETH. All those dusty roads, dozens of them. Look how they twist and turn and cross each other . . .
RACHEL. It's a strange light . . . it will rain soon, won't it?
JAPHETH. (*Soberly.*) Very soon. . . .
RACHEL. (*Hesitantly.*) Japheth . . . don't you think the ark needs you?
JAPHETH. Poppa doesn't think so.
RACHEL. Yes, he does, but you'd have to bend a little.
JAPHETH. My bending days are over. Goodbye, Rachel. (*He walks toward his baggage. After a hesitant pause she steps toward him.*)
RACHEL. What do you want to stay behind for . . . ?
JAPHETH. For what I believe in?
RACHEL. (*With a new doggedness.*) What do you believe in?
JAPHETH. (*Crosses D. L. C. Promptly.*) Those roads down there!

The patterns they make! They're not cobwebs, those roads, the work of a foolish spider, to be brushed away by a peevish boy! Those roads were made by men, men crazy not to be alone or apart! Men, crazy to reach other! (*Pausing with bitter sadness.*) Well, they won't now. . . .
RACHEL. Japheth, this sounds wrong to me. If you think people should reach each other . . . the ark is the only place they'll do it now.
JAPHETH. (*Impatiently.*) Rachel, you won't make me change my mind.
RACHEL. (*Crosses to him. Earnestly.*) Japheth, I beg you to think! There is idealism now in just survival!
JAPHETH. I don't think you can convince me, Rachel—
RACHEL. (*At a turning point in her life.*) I can't?
JAPHETH. No.
RACHEL. You'll stay behind. . . .
JAPHETH. Yes, Because even if you convinced me, what about us?
RACHEL. What about us?
JAPHETH. I love you and couldn't live and work beside you on the ark!
RACHEL. (*Trying to stop him. Crosses away* R.) Japheth, please—!
JAPHETH. I love you and—
RACHEL. —Please don't.
JAPHETH. And I can't remember the time I didn't!
RACHEL. (*Crying out.*) I don't want to hear it now— (*Looking squarely at him.*) You're not inspired by your love for your mother or me. You're inspired by your pain, and it's vile. (*She turns away, beside herself, putting her shaking hands to her face. Crosses* U. *ramp. He has turned and looks out tightly at the valley.*)
JAPHETH. (*Abruptly.*) Look at those birds go! (*His head whips around and returns quickly to face the valley.*)
RACHEL. They're frightened. . . .
JAPHETH. Look at the clouds. . . .
RACHEL. They're moving. . . .
JAPHETH. (*Calling loudly.*) Poppa!
RACHEL. Look at the dust flying!
JAPHETH. Poppa!
RACHEL. Where did the wind come from suddenly.
JAPHETH. (*Tightly.*) From the bosom of God's infinite mercy . . .

(*Then, turning.*) There! (*Noah appears, followed by Shem and a moment later, Esther. The others all appear, too, Goldie, the last, cowering behind, scarcely able to walk. Japheth merely points the situation to his father; for a moment everyone looks in stomach-sickened silence. Finally Noah speaks, awe-struck:*)
NOAH. The grass blows . . . the wind shakes the dust . . . it's the end of the world . . . (*Then, briskly.*) Shem, all the animals are on board?
SHEM. (*Awed.*) Everything alive is on board, yes sir.
NOAH. It looks close . . . (*Then.*) Esther, tuchter, don't excite yourself. Get everything ready. The Lord waits an' watches. (*Noah puts an arm around Esther, but he slowly drops it when he [and the others] see that she has her eyes only on Japheth. Noah gashes the matter with a crisp command.*) Awright, boys, everything on board—chairs, tables, whatsoever!
LEAH. Girls, come on! The olive oil, the jars, the jars, the loom—don't forget the loom!
SHEM. And the cornmeal! Poppa, there's more stuff than we think!
NOAH. We'll all give a hand . . . get it on! (*Everyone goes to work with the zeal and appearance of the participants of a picnic interrupted by a storm. Meanwhile the Old Men have appeared again, the Old Man approaching Noah with tentative steps. Esther and Japheth have not moved; Goldie, in the background, has started for the ark with a bundle, her gait so uncertain that for a moment it seems she won't complete her task.*)
OLD MAN. Take us, Noah . . . take us with you.
NOAH. (*Gently but firmly.*) This an' only this is His orders, the family, brother. Please, please don't ask me again. (*Everyone is impressed by a silent flash of deep lightning.*)
OLD MAN. We know the Old Law. Take one of us . . .
NOAH. (*Shaking his head.*) Please don't ast me again.
OLD MAN. We know the Old Law behind the Old Law—it will be forgotten. (*Each Old Man says of the other, "Take him, take him," etc. Esther steps in with assistance.*)
ESTHER. He would like to do it in the worst way, but he dasn't. (*Disappointed, the Old Men retire to* D. L. *where soon they will begin to chant and intone old Hebrew prayers until the very end of the scene. Noah calls to Shem who is hurrying out* U. L.)
NOAH. Shem, the animal feed! (*Shem and Ham cross* R. *to* L.)

SHEM. That's what I'm picking up right now! (*Now Noah is left free to face Japheth, Esther behind him.*)
NOAH. Japheth, I won't fight. You'll go on board, like a decent respectable boy.
JAPHETH. (*Quietly.*) I'm s-staying behind.
NOAH. You'll sail on the ark . . . (*Japheth shakes his head stubbornly. There is another flash of lightning, this time with two tails. The returning Goldie falls to her knees. Esther goes to her, Noah turning inquiringly.*) God arranged it for you—you took a wife. Now go on the ark—you'll start a new life.
JAPHETH. (*White-faced.*) I'll say goodbye, Poppa. (*Shem calls urgently, passing through from* L. *to* R., *a bag of feed on his back:*)
SHEM. Poppa, you'll have to give a hand— (*Meanwhile Esther has helped Goldie to a seat. The sky is growing increasingly darker, a wind is beginning to stir the palm trees, their dry leaves scraping, some dust and rubbish flying. Antiphonal roosters are heard in the distance and in a little time crickets will begin to chirp, as during a solar eclipse.*)
NOAH. You go right in the ark! I'll tell you once again it's God's orders—!
JAPHETH. I'm not obeying orders!
ESTHER. (*Anger arriving.*) But then you'll die in the water! What're you talking about?
JAPHETH. I'd rather die in protest, Momma, than live.
ESTHER. Protest?—that's foolish! You think you know what's right? So have your own sons an' teach them! (*More lightning, with thunder coming up behind it, the wind increasing its velocity. Leah is in and out with her arms full, Shem hurries by, Rachel with him, momentarily stopped by the quarrel.*)
JAPHETH. (*Protestingly.*) But, listen, Poppa— I—
NOAH. (*Enraged.*) No more, I warn you, the power of God is in my arm.
JAPHETH. What I'm trying to— (*Words stop coming out of Japheth's mouth because Noah in one blow knocks him senseless to the ground.*)
NOAH. (*Breathing heavily.*) Please, Lord, forgive him. Put his sins on my body. (*Turning.*) Shem, carry him on the ark. Take him down below. (*Ham having just advanced into the scene, he and Shem carry Japheth away in silence, for a moment only a soft*

sobbing from Goldie and the sounds of nature are heard. Noah starts out U. L., saying to Rachel as he passes her:) Start movin', time is short. *(Saying "Yes," Rachel goes about her business. In a moment Noah will go from L. to R. with a sack on his back and Shem and Ham, returning from the ark will do likewise. Meanwhile Esther is left alone with Goldie and her thoughts.)*

ESTHER. Don't be afraid now—you'll go on the ark.

GOLDIE. *(Pallidly.)* But you don't know anything about me . . .

ESTHER. *(Stolidly.)* So you'll tell me some day.

GOLDIE. Please, I've got to tell you right now.

ESTHER. *(Sharply.)* Who you were I don't care, hear me? But who you'll be, I care very much!

GOLDIE. But I must tell you the truth—!

ESTHER. Excuse me, the truth isn't the truth right now! It's a big luxury we can't afford! Hear me! *(She has gripped the girl's arms and seems to shake some tone back into her, for Goldie says, "Yes, yes . . .")* Now don't stand on ceremony an' give a hand . . . *(The atmosphere has turned an angry yellow gray. Esther goes to where Leah and Rachel are handling small olive oil jars and helps them. Goldie, with a new lease on life, joins them in bringing the jars to the base of the ramp where Shem and Ham take them onto the ark. It is Shem who sticks out a hand and calls loudly:)*

SHEM. Rain!

ESTHER. Rain . . . ?

SHEM. Rain, everybody, rain! *(Every member of the family slowly clumps together, an awed hush.)*

NOAH. Rain . . .

HAM. Big drops . . . look down that valley!

SHEM. *(Incredulously.)* Is that rain . . . ?

LEAH. *(Shading her eyes.)* Sheets . . . curtains . . .

NOAH. The roads is awready small rivers!

SHEM. Those birds are flying for their life!

NOAH. Go, boys, make sure everything's closed up good, windows, doors . . . *(The two sons hurry to their tasks; Noah makes a brisk inspection tour of the "premises." Rachel nervously draws closer to Esther who already has Goldie on the other side of her; Leah leans against the ramp in the background.)*

RACHEL. It's coolin' off very quick.

ESTHER. Don't be nervous, Rachel, but if you wanna cry, cry . . . (*Then.*) Where's Leah?
LEAH. Here.
ESTHER. (*Dryly.*) I thought we lost you. (*A medley of creature sounds is heard from the ark: clucking, whistling, grunts and roars sliced by snarls. The three Old Men stand at* L. *in a beseeching way. Noah is jogging an odd bale of hay up the ramp and from there looks out at the weird scene, calling from there.*)
NOAH. Everyone should stay on the ark. It's gettin' dark—we don't know what could happen.
ESTHER. Go, girls . . . (*Rachel and Goldie start for the ramp, Esther meanwhile is looking around vaguely.*) I know I forgot something, but what . . . ? (*Shem takes the bale from Noah's hands and pulls it up on board. Noah comes down and in a certain very courtly way takes Esther' arm. The children are watching from the deck.*)
NOAH. Come, old friend, I'll help you . . . to your new home . . . (*Esther's mood is strange, for she wants to both laugh and cry.*)
ESTHER. (*Then, looking.*) What did I forget . . . ? Noah, my heart is in my mouth. . . .
NOAH. (*Face furrowed with pain.*) My hands is cold as ice can be . . .
ESTHER. (*Finally, sighing deeply, she permits him to lead her towards the ark but abruptly she pulls away, saying:*) The hat! My hat! (*As she goes* R. *to pick up the hat, Noah abruptly cries:*)
NOAH. What did I forget? The gitka! The little gitka! (*He goes* R. *and at the base of the tree picks up the precious sawdust box in which the gitka lives. Then he and Esther start for the ramp together again. The children watch them with humorless faces, Goldie and Rachel are weeping softly. Lightning, thunder and denser rain now. The Old Men are chanting aloud, their unbowed heads beginning to drip like running candles. The boys reach down to help their mother up, but Noah stays on the ground and looks out again, this time looking upward.*) For the last time, oh Lord, must it be . . . ? (*As if in answer, the world seems to shake with thunder. Noah sobs aloud, blinded alike by tears and rain. Shem steps down and takes his arm, saying in a choked voice:*)
SHEM. Come, Poppa. . . . (*Noah lets himself be led like a*

child. *More lashing electricity in the air. The Old Men are stone fixtures in the dripping landscape. An appalling atmosphere.)*

CURTAIN

SCENE 6

On board the ark.
Music continues after curtain rises. It is dawn. Finally, Noah is discovered seated, looking out at the waters, the gitka on his lap. He sighs deeply and speaks:

NOAH. The world was so beautiful, so REAL . . . now it's one big damn, sucked-down hole. Yeh, God's workin' it out just like he said. . . . (*As the gitka begins to sing.*) Sing, gitka, sing . . . don't you be scared, 'cause I'm here . . . (*Noah listens to the gitka for a moment, it sings for a little time after he begins to talk.*) I'm thinkin' back a good many years . . . my father's father, Methusaleh (Ah, a wonder for the world he was!), he knew I was born for something special—what you call a BIG JOB! "Go out, Noah, go out an' preach repentance to the world!" Yeh, that was the story! (*Sighing.*) What should I tell you . . . ? Evil is a stone wall. . . . I hurt my head a lotta times! She'll tell you, my Esther—I slept with her in one bed for SIXTY YEARS! Worries, troubles, couldn't meet my bills, couldn't sleep—I began to drink! I started to go down! (*Pausing, sorrowfully.*) My name became no good. . . . (*Then, with tender awe.*) But God Almighty, blessed be His name, He found me out and give me back my good name to some extent . . . (*With holiness.*) Yeh, here's me an' there's that miserable no-good, lonely wild world out there . . . hurts me . . . (*Then standing.*) You'll go downstairs, girlie . . . tell them it's the forty-first day . . . the big rains is over. (*Noah puts the gitka in one door as Japheth emerges from the other, some poles, tools and wash lines in his hands. The young man looks out at the water with awe. Noah turns and says:*) Japheth? You're up so early?
JAPHETH. (*Looking out, to himself.*) The rain is over. . . .
NOAH. Yeh, the poor wood must be cryin' to be so wet. You're

fixing something? (*Waiting.*) I ast you a question. . . . (*Japheth is definitely unfriendly, despite Noah's appeasing manner.*)
JAPHETH. Momma wants to hang some wash later.
NOAH. (*As his son works.*) You're still mad at me? Maybe some day, sonny, you'll thank me for takin' you on the Ark. (*Then.*) Now, what about Goldie? You talked to her yet?
JAPHETH. (*Curtly.*) No and I don't intend to.
NOAH. (*Surprised.*) Whhhy . . . ?
JAPHETH. Because, just like you, I'm an independent man and I don't want her.
NOAH. (*Huffily.*) Next I guess you'll start with the rudder?
JAPHETH. Yes, I'll say anything that's on my mind. You can always lock me up again. (*Silence: The men's feud glitters between them. Noah hawks and splits before saying quietly:*)
NOAH. Why is the ark slanty?
JAPHETH. (*At work.*) Some cargo must've shifted—I'll look later.
NOAH. What's this I hear we have no snails on board . . . ?
JAPHETH. We have one, the murmex snail.
NOAH. But what good is one?
JAPHETH. With snails the he is a he AND a she.
NOAH. (*Astonished.*) He's a she? A he AND a she? Lucky person! (*Then.*) Sonny, it's an honor to you how you took care— (*He turns and is surprised to find that Japheth has drifted to the other side of the housing with his tools.*) Went away? Looks to me like a good boy, but I dunno . . . (*He turns away musingly, Shem enters from the other door.*)
SHEM. It's a holy time . . . the rains are over . . . good morning, Poppa . . . (*Then, sighing.*) knock on wood, how this ark stood up I'll never know.
NOAH. (*Austerely.*) An' don't you worry, it's not over yet. We'll float around the best part of a year. And only God knows where!
SHEM. (*Ruminating.*) Did you ever realize, Poppa, when we land —granting all goes well—that the whole world will be ours?
NOAH. (*With a dour chuckle.*) Ours? Awright, whatever you'll grow with your own hands, it's yours. People you can't hire no more to work for you.
SHEM. Yeah, that's what worries me . . .
NOAH. (*With sad outrage.*) The whole world stinks of ruined bodies an' rotten grass. And today, Shem, on this sacred wood, your head's fulla business . . . ?

SHEM. Poppa, sir, I give emphatic prayer and thanks! But later, sir, you'll admit, it behooves us all to use our God-given brains.
NOAH. (*Angrily.*) No, I don't hit with this talk! You're awready workin' how to take from your brothers an' your brother's children! (*Shem is glad to be able to divert the subject to the working sounds behind the housing.*)
SHEM. Who is that?
NOAH. (*Gloomily.*) Japheth's FIXIN'.
SHEM. He still mad?
NOAH. Lemons would make him sweeter!
SHEM. (*Smooth and judicious.*) Yeah, but it's lucky he's with us. Because if we run into trouble—
NOAH. Don't have a big mouth like your mother, 'cause I'm here! If we love the Lord we won't have troubles! Something's in my mind with you an' Ham—watch out for yourself, you fresh man! (*He turns and walks away, shaking his fist at the sky as he says:*) And Lilith black angel of the night—she's in the air, too! Don't you come near the ark, girlie! (*Ham enters; he is drunk and stumbles; Shem immediately trying to pull him to one side.*)
HAM. Damn this tipsy ark!
SHEM. (*Warningly.*) Hold your mouth, willya!
HAM. (*Pulling loose.*) What're you pulling? (*Then.*) Well, a clear day!
NOAH. (*Eyeing him sternly.*) Just how I thought—you're drunk! I seen the situation a week awready—Shem gives you liquor to do his work? You made it, from the family dates?
SHEM. (*Sullenly, after a pause.*) I brought a keg on board for the holidays.
NOAH. I'll begin to cry in a minute. (*With a painful roar.*) Both of you—an' Japheth, too!—your name's gettin' worser to me by the minute! Maybe he'll tell me some day why He picked this family. (*Shaking his head, Noah turns and goes below. Ham sniggers nervously and Shem turns angrily to him:*)
SHEM. Did you have to open your big yap? (*Indignantly.*) I started to tell him how brains are needed for the future, for reconstruction—
HAM. (*Slyly.*) You were looking ahead?
SHEM. (*Annoyed.*) I'm always looking ahead, willya! All the land is ours, I said. And my brain, I said—

HAM. (*Laughing.*) What brain? There isn't a sound apple in your barrel!

SHEM. (*Promptly.*) You're drunk!

HAM. You stand there reconstructing the world and I'm drunk? Down below, eldest son, your shovel waits!

SHEM. You owe me three weeks more. (*Ham laughs in his face and Shem steps in, as if to take him by the throat, instead he starts out stopping to say:*)

HAM. Ha!

SHEM. I'll always buy a man like you . . . I'll always have something you need, that's why. And I'll invent it with my head—right here on the ark, TOO! (*The light has advanced upward from dawn. It is becoming like morning. Alone, Ham crows and laughs happily, rubbing his hands. Japheth meanwhile has been marooned in the background. He is about to step out but Rachel appears in one of the doorways and he must remain a reluctant witness.*)

HAM. Well, what's up mouse, looking for a cat? (*Rachel flicks a look at him and turns to look out at the watery world.*) Awesome ain't it?

RACHEL. I thank God that I'm alive. Momma sent me up. She wants to hang some wash after breakfast.

HAM. Listen, what's happening here? I can't fluster you any more. You are changing.

RACHEL. If we don't change on the Holy Ark where will we change?

HAM. Oh, shut up. Just shut up with that stuff! An' by the way, what are you doing sleeping over in Momma's room?

RACHEL. She wants it that way and I'm sorry to say so do I.

HAM. Funny to relate I don't care what you do. I care what Goldie does. Japheth won't marry her.

RACHEL. Ham, I could never live with you again.

HAM. (*Tauntingly.*) That's a lot to say in one little remark.

RACHEL. (*Almost defiantly.*) I've said it.

HAM. I'm wonderin' about hittin' you, but it's my day off. I'll go down below and wash. Maybe I'll do some fishin' later. (*Snickering he leaves the deck. His brutal attitude has not been easy for Rachel to take. Trying to leave the deck unnoticed Japheth drops a tool. When Rachel sees him she quickly sits and with shame puts her face in her hands.*)

JAPHETH. I didn't mean to listen, but I was stuck there. (*Stop-*

ping abruptly.) Why do we keep hiding from each other? We've exhausted every nook and cranny on the ark. Now you're hiding behind your hands. Rachel, why don't we face the facts.
RACHEL. (*She slowly lifts her head but does not look at him.*) What are the facts . . . ?
JAPHETH. We love each other . . . I won't marry Goldie.
RACHEL. Is it right for us to discuss these things?
JAPHETH. (*Impatiently.*) Why not, if they're facts?
RACHEL. Japheth, don't be harsh.
JAPHETH. Rachel, I love you and want to marry you.
RACHEL. (*Troubled.*) I would marry you . . . but your father won't permit it.
JAPHETH. Ham was right—you're changing. Well, I'm changing, too— And my father—innocent and stubborn as he is— HE'LL have to change!
RACHEL. All my life I've been afraid—
JAPHETH. You mustn't be afraid— I'll make you strong!
RACHEL. (*Stirred.*) Japheth, you're right! I look around . . . what else can happen? Thank you, thank you, Japheth, that you need me—
JAPHETH. (*Gently.*) Let me kiss you, Rachel, here in God's clear air . . .
RACHEL. (*Shyly again.*) Yes . . . (*At this moment Esther enters from the other side followed by Goldie and Leah each with a basket of wash. The three women are impressed by the looks of the clear but overcast world. On the other side of the deck Rachel and Japheth break apart unseen by the others.*)
GOLDIE. Nothing to see, nothing.
ESTHER. (*Looking to the deck.*) I wonder why the ark is cockeyed? Maybe that's what my husband's so mad about. (*Esther crosses R. and sees the young couple. Their attitude tells her much.*)
JAPHETH. Good morning Momma.
ESTHER. Good morning, children. Poppa wants you downstairs, Japhie. (*He nods, looking significantly at Rachel and goes below. Rachel looks embarrassed.*) You're looking very good today Rachel but take a piece of advice, keep your hands busy and later we'll have a talk.
RACHEL. Yes, I will. Thank you, Momma. I'll help hang the wash. (*She joins the other girls who are busy filling the lines with damp clothes. Esther cocks an eye at the sky and says, sighing:*)

ESTHER. If the sun comes out I will be a happy woman. I'm easy to satisfy, God. (*Crosses* U. R. *behind cabin. Ham returns with a fishing line and walks to the bow. Meanwhile, Shem emerges from* L. *with a pair of slop buckets in his hands. He calls in a sharp, low tone to Leah and she joins him immediately.*)
SHEM. Leah, where's the key?
LEAH. Under the mat.
SHEM. The door's locked tight?
LEAH. Yes. (*Shem goes to an unseen spot where he dumps the pails and returns below. Esther drifts into sight again. She shakes her head as she looks at the sky. Crosses* D. L.)
ESTHER. I must be out of my mind. Sun we won't see today. Where is my brains? Girls, we'd better take it all downstairs again. Go, make the fire bigger, Leah. We can dry the small things by the kitchen stove. Ham, give Leah a hand. She needs extra firewood.
HAM. (*Annoyed.*) This is my day off, Momma.
ESTHER. Go, it only takes a minute. (*Calling.*) Girls! Goldie? (*Crosses* U. L. *behind cabin. Leah goes below while Esther drifts toward the back. Ham leisurely starts for a doorway and meets Goldie coming around from the right. They drop their voices.*)
HAM. Hello snake. I'm waitin' to be constricted to death nice and slow.
GOLDIE. You'll wait a long time, lad.
HAM. Are you sure? (*Goldie smiles as she passes Ham and joins Esther and Rachel.*)
RACHEL. Leave the sheets?
ESTHER. (*Crosses* D. L.) Leave the sheets. (*Noah enters* R. *and crosses to stern with Esther's plant. Esther, crosses* C.) Where you taking my plant?
NOAH. It needs sun, tuchter, like everything else.
ESTHER. (*Dryly. Sits bench* C.) Where's sun, Noah?
NOAH. (*Surprised.*) I seen you puttin' out wash, I didn't look. . . .
ESTHER. Weeks awready we can't dry a wash. My arms are fallin' off. . . .
NOAH. God didn't speak to me in a big long time. I'm worried, but no news is good news. (*Then.*) Leviathan, the whale, he didn't die in the flood. Oh, no, not that mean sucker. (*To himself.*) I miss meself a little drink now and then. (*To Esther.*) Esther, I'm

worried. . . . (*Sits R. of her. She seems to ignore this remark as she picks up a palm leaf fan and says with mild interest:*)
ESTHER. Look, my plant took a new leaf— I didn't notice.
NOAH. (*Rather sharply.*) Esther, I'm talkin' to you!
ESTHER. So where am I, in Egypt . . . ?
NOAH. Don't make fun. I'm tellin' you for weeks already—they should git married! The world needs babies!
ESTHER. Goldie an' Japhie—?
NOAH. Should git married! She's in one room—he's next door—it's not nice! It gives the ark a bad name! (*Pausing.*) And I'll ast you again—what's Rachel livin' in our bedroom, sleepin' in my bed with you?
ESTHER. Oh, you, don't you get so fresh, you!
NOAH. (*Prancing.*) This is fresh by you? A woman I slept with her in one bed for sixty years—suddenly I'm sleepin' on the couch. Whhhy . . . ?
ESTHER. Do me a favor, Noah, an' don't bother me, hey?
NOAH. (*Inexpressibly shocked.*) This is how you talk to me? (*Very hurt.*) Honest, why should the boys listen to me . . .? (*Then, turned away.*) You'll look into this matter, Esther—Rachel shall go back to Ham. (*She has turned her back. He snuffles and walks away softly, but hearing a sound he turns and looks at her back: she is crying! Wonderingly.*) Esther . . .? You're cryin'? (*He walks to her and sees that she is really crying and is immediately filled with love, awe and consternation.*)
ESTHER. Go 'way from me. . . .
NOAH. My Esther is cryin' . . . ?! . . .
ESTHER. (*Crying.*) Whatta you want from me, Noah? I'm a tired old woman . . . you're a young man . . .
NOAH. You're my wife, Esther, for sixty years. . . .
ESTHER. (*Sadly, shaking her head.*) No, no more . . . an old lady, like your mother. . . .
NOAH. (*Sparking up.*) Don't you ever forget, girlie, it's a big knot, a helluva, how we're tied together!
ESTHER. No . . .
NOAH. Yeh!
ESTHER. (*Recovering herself.*) It's a mess, but what could you do . . .
NOAH. No . . .
ESTHER. Yeh . . .

NOAH. You're feeling better, old friend . . . ?
SHEM. (*Appears* L. *with two more buckets.*) Excuse me, Momma.
ESTHER. Excused. (*Wryly.*) Yeh, but you'll do me a favor, Noah
. . . sleep on the couch. . . . (*She has meanwhile picked up several pieces of wash and goes below. Esther gone, Noah at the bow, hawks and spits overboard reflectively, shaking his head and seeming to argue with himself. Shem, with a glance at his father's back, goes about the business of waste disposal, Ham comes out of the hatchway and meets him returning.*)
HAM. Among other things, why are you locking your door these days?
SHEM. I deplore these insinuations. What do you mean?
HAM. Japheth's on the prowl, you know, and very good at unlocking doors.
SHEM. (*Stiffening.*) What door?
HAM. *Your* door, brown eyes . . . (*Shem goes pell-mell. Ham smiles smoothly and approaches his father.*) Hello, Pops, thinking about big things . . . ?
NOAH. I'm looking for you! (*Ham turns with a surprised gesture of "Here I am."*) What's between you an' Rachel?
HAM. Nothing's between us.
NOAH. But God is watching for what He wants . . . followin' me what I mean?
HAM. Sure, to raise families. But I'm no magician, with my wife over in Momma's room! (*Noah is now wishing he hadn't brought the matter up, but he says, with typical incongruous daintiness.*)
NOAH. Your Rachel, she's a decent, respectable girl—
HAM. (*Slyly.*) But *is* she? She's in love with Japheth. . . .
NOAH. (*Pausing, narrowly.*) An' Japheth . . . ?
HAM. (*Shrugging.*) Your true adulterer is a stealthy man . . . who knows?
NOAH. It's solid facts? You know it . . . ? (*Noah is looking so piercingly at Ham that he drops his eyes and turns away, attempting to fumigate the tense atmosphere with a laugh.*)
HAM. Come on, Poppa, don't take everything so serious! (*He again drops his eyes, Noah speaks with a strong, hushed bitterness.*)
NOAH. It's a thing of pity, what you'll joke about . . . (*Walking away, shaking his head.*) an' I knew you for a little bit of a baby . . (*Returning.*) I'll speak to Rachel—she'll go back to you.

(*Meanwhile an altercation has been building up below, and it now spills itself out on the deck in the guise of a determined Japheth and Shem, who enter* R., *followed by Leah and Goldie.*)

ESTHER. (*Enters* L.) The steps are killing me.

JAPHETH. Take your hands off me, Shem! Don't hold me! . . .
(*Shem, who has been trying to stop Japheth, desists when he sees Noah, the scene slows to a cautious walk.*)

NOAH. (*Turning.*) What's a matter, here . . . ?

SHEM. Nothing, Poppa. (*Noah fixes them with his piercing look, flicking a side glance at Ham.*)

NOAH. (*Crisply.*) Maybe you lost the sense for it, so I'll tell you all—the ark is a temple! An' each an' every one, we live in the service of the Lord: He's Boss over me an' I'm boss over you, yeh: The way it begins to stand there's better ones in the water than here on the deck! Rachel, go down in my room—bring me back my "tallis," my prayer shawl.

ESTHER. For what?

NOAH. (*Of Goldie and Japheth.*) I'll marry them.

ESTHER. When?

NOAH. Now, this minute! (*Rachel is unable to move, Esther steps out.*)

ESTHER. She don't know where to find your prayer shawl, the good one— I put it away with camphor.

NOAH. So the old one, next to the silver spoons.

ESTHER. Noah—!

NOAH. Never mind, I'll go myself. (*Bristling with command, Noah goes to the companionway and, looking back briefly, goes below. Rachel sits as if stunned, Esther putting a comforting hand on her shoulder. Japheth walks front and looks out at the water with a bleak face. Goldie, looking from one to the other, breaks the silence first.*)

GOLDIE. Why is everyone so unhappy? I want to cry, too, but I've never been married before! (*No one means to be unkind, but Goldie is left unanswered.*)

SHEM. In my considered opinion, Poppa is completely right. In unstable times respect for authority must prevail.

JAPHETH. (*Turning.*) Are you lunatic? Is this the time for you to deliver sermons? Momma, why do you think the ark is tipped?

SHEM. (*Quickly.*) Now just a minute, young man—!

JAPHETH. (*To Esther.*) He's endangering the life of everyone on board! He and his wife—they're hoarding!
SHEM. This is not the time—!
JAPHETH. Shem, for your own sake, let me finish before Poppa returns! (*To Esther.*) The stuff is stacked to the ceiling—
ESTHER. (*Puzzled.*) What stuff?
JAPHETH. Maybe two thousand pounds of it—that's why the ark is lopsided! *Manure!*
ESTHER. (*Baffled.*) Manure . . . ! (*Abruptly Noah is back with blood in his eye; he walks directly to Shem and looks at him in frigid silence before asking:*)
NOAH. I seen your door was open . . . what's that stuff?
ESTHER. Manure . . .
NOAH. Manure I seen, but for what? The ark shall turn upside down for manure?
SHEM. (*Sullenly.*) It's not manure. It's dried manure briquettes —fuel.
LEAH. Fuel for the future!
SHEM. When we land there won't be a piece of dry fuel—
HAM. Except his briquettes!
SHEM. (*Aggrieved.*) All I was doing was looking ahead—
HAM. To the time he can sell us something we all have to buy!
NOAH. (*Pausing.*) On the holy ark he's makin' business! Manure! With manure you want to begin a new world? Everybody's life he put in danger!
ESTHER. Poppa's a hundred percent right.
NOAH. (*Harshly.*) You'll dump it overboard right away! (*Esther begins to navigate a little.*)
ESTHER. If you made it to sell, Shem, you're a low dog! But if you made it for the family—
SHEM. (*Picking up the cue.*) But, Momma, that's what I did—I made it for the family!
ESTHER. (*Pretending surprise.*) You hear, Noah?
NOAH. (*Suspiciously.*) Esther, you shouldn't take his part, hear me?
ESTHER. But if it's for the family, why throw it overboard . . . ? (*Noah looks at her, aware that she is putting something over on him; he turns away with tight lips, hands behind his back. Esther, stolidly.*) Shem made a useful thing from nothing, yeh? Why kill

the man with brains? No, make him use it for the *family!* (*Innocently.*) I said it right, Noah . . . ?

NOAH. (*Mutteringly.*) Go 'way from me. . . . (*Noah starts towards the bow, muttering to himself, but, remembering, turns and starts back. Meanwhile Leah has quietly slipped below after a few whispered words with Shem.*) I didn't forget what I started to do. Go downstairs, Japheth—get my prayer shawl.

JAPHETH. (*Pausing.*) I'm not marrying Goldie . . .

NOAH. (*Glittering.*) Be careful, sonny!

JAPHETH. I want to marry Rachel. Ham has left her.

HAM. (*Quickly.*) She left *me!* (*Japheth walks over to Rachel who has risen to her feet.*)

JAPHETH. They're living apart . . . we love each other. (*Noah looks, blinks, cranes his neck; it is more than he can grasp for a moment.*)

ESTHER. Noah, what he means to say—

NOAH. (*Harshly, silencing her.*) I'm here, ain't I? (*On second thought.*) Or ain't I . . . ? (*He pauses, looking around rather wildly before asking:*) And Ham . . . ?

ESTHER. Would like to marry Goldie. . . .

HAM. (*Hastily.*) I didn't say that, Poppa!

NOAH. Whatever you're saying, all of you, it's a thing I hate it as well as I hate murder! The ark is a holy temple!

ESTHER. (*Doggedly.*) No, it's a stable—around the clock a Turkish bath for animals! People are wore out from work an' misery! (*Noah is baffled—can Esther be on the side of such impiety?*)

NOAH. (*Warningly.*) You'll go so far, the whole bunch, but don't you go too far!

SHEM. Yeah, Poppa's right! (*Shem steps away from the others and aligns himself with Noah.*)

NOAH. (*Emphatically.*) Where marriage an' divorce is concerned, it says in the rules an' regulations, from way back—!

ESTHER. (*Impatiently.*) But since "way back" people are changing, Noah!

NOAH. (*Writhing.*) No, girlie, He didn't destroy the whole world, the Awmighty, to find all the sins on the ark! (*Exploding.*) Esther, you don't see—you're blind? *They don't stop acting like human beings!!*

JAPHETH. God had to pick human beings to help Him, didn't

He? Now, if He doesn't like it that human beings act like human beings, He's out of luck!
NOAH. (*Engorged.*) Who's outa luck?!
ESTHER. God's outa luck . . . and you'll hit me first. (*It looks for a moment as if, eyes bulging, Noah will strike Esther for the first time in his life. Shem stirs uneasily, murmuring, "Poppa. . . ." Then Noah's elan seems to puff away and he speaks next from a remote, empty point.*)
NOAH. I don't wanna see it! I can't look!
ESTHER. (*Startled.*) What's the matter?
NOAH. This very minute God will strike them right down on the deck, the whole bunch! I don't wanna see. (*The people look at each other, a few uneasily. Noah scarcely dares look around and finally asks in a whisper.*) They're still alive, the hateable persons . . . ?
ESTHER. (*Dryly.*) Nothing happened, Noah. (*Noah turns very slowly and is both astonished and nonplussed to find the human situation unchanged, not to mention a little humiliated.*)
NOAH. Maybe God bent down to tie his shoelace— He didn't see them. But don't you worry. He's only tuning up—the real music didn't begin yet. (*Controlling his trembling voice.*) And you, Esther, old friend of mine, you left me. For the first time in sixty years—you went away from me! I'll go cover my head— I'll cry 'til God's judgment comes.
GOLDIE. (*Anxiously.*) What'll happen now . . . ? (*Esther appears with a wearied shrug. Abruptly the rich late afternoon sun comes out in a swollen blaze.*)
HAM. Sun!
RACHEL. Sun . . .
ESTHER. Sun . . . (*Sighing.*) Tomorrow we'll scrub the ark from top to bottom. . . . (*She starts heavily for the companionway. Leah has just come up and joined Shem and is whispering something to him. Japheth and Rachel have joined each other in the bow. Ham has sidled over to Goldie.*)
HAM. Snake, dear, we're established.
GOLDIE. Wait and see. (*He whispers into her ear. Esther has stopped half in and half out of the hatchway. She has been seized with a pain so intense that she holds on with one hand while the other clutches at her stomach. At this moment Shem detaches himself from Leah, saying:*)

SHEM. I better go look. (*He walks to the hatchway and is surprised to see his mother standing there; she shows him nothing.*) Momma!— Something the matter?
ESTHER. A pain—
SHEM. Leah tells me . . . Poppa took the brandy from my room, the whole keg.
ESTHER. (*Struck.*) Brandy? Stay here. I'll go see. I took your part—but don't make a mistake, children, Noah *is* my favorite boy.

CURTAIN

SCENE 7

Late at night. Weeks later. An exhausted Japheth is alone on deck, seated at the rudder. Shem and Ham enter R.

JAPHETH. Shem . . . ?
SHEM. Yeah.
JAPHETH. Nothing new below?
SHEM. No. We can't find him. Either he's hiding or he's overboard. (*Ham has walked to the side and is looking overboard.*)
HAM. What do you think we hit?
JAPHETH. (*Yawning.*) It looked like part of a house to me.
SHEM. (*To Japheth, with gloomy exasperation.*) What are you so calm about? Momma's sick, Poppa's maybe overboard, the ark has sprung a leak—!
JAPHETH. The ark is still afloat. And Poppa, if you ask me, isn't overboard.
SHEM. (*Lapsing.*) What do you think we should do?
JAPHETH. Wait another hour till daylight. Anyway, I can't finish the repairs in the dark. I'm cold, and tired, too.
SHEM. I'll bring you up a hot drink. I'm in a mood to weep. (*Going.*) I don't know where we'd be without you, boy . . . (*He exits, preceded by Ham. Next, from the other side, a sober but worn out Noah enters. Father and son are not aware of each other until Noah speaks.*)
NOAH. It's night or it's day . . . ? (*Rubbing himself, then, humbly, arms lifted.*) God, You lifted me. You made me for a

man of big trust . . . I disappointed You . . . I'm down to the bottom again . . . (*Seeming to weep for a moment before lifting his arms again.*) Months aweready I didn't hear from You, Honorable Sir. I can't do this job by myself . . . why don't you tell the boys they're wrong? (*With tender pleading.*) God, a man is small—bend down an' talk in his ear! (*Waiting, baffled.*) You can't make Him come out if He don't wanna. . . .
JAPHETH. (*Softly.*) Poppa. . . .
NOAH. (*Startled.*) Who's 'at . . . ?
JAPHETH. I'm glad to see you, Poppa. Everyone's been very worried about you—even thought you went overboard.
NOAH. Too bad about them! What's this? YOU'RE STEERING THE ARK! (*Crosses to him.*)
JAPHETH. (*Nodding.*) And standing night watch, too. We hit some big floating object last night—part of a house it looked.
NOAH. (*Angrily.*) You're running the ark now?
JAPHETH. (*Picking up his tone.*) You've been drunk for nine weeks, sir.
NOAH. (*A wincing whisper.*) Nine . . . nine! (*Then briskly.*) God never said we should steer the ark! Tomorrow first thing you'll take it off!
JAPHETH. (*Temper slipping.*) And God didn't tell you to invent the hoe and the rake and yet you did!
NOAH. (*Flatly.*) I was a youngster then—what did I know? If you'll ast me today, I'm sorry I done it!
JAPHETH. (*Incredulously.*) Sorry? You said sorry?
NOAH. (*Fiercely.*) Yeh, yeh, yeh! It made work too easy an' people for loafers!
JAPHETH. Not so loud please— Momma's sick downstairs.
NOAH. (*Haughtily.*) Last night I seen her, never mind. Who do you think I stopped drinkin' for? You? (*A few unhappy asides.*) I'm altogether in a lonely sorta way. I slept many times with the cows the last weeks—sweet persons. Maybe we were saved for the animals, not ourself. (*Then.*) I'll go down an' see Mother, but she don't want me . . . (*Japheth picks up this last remark and abruptly both men are at it hammer and tongs!*)
JAPHETH. That's foolish.
NOAH. (*Turning.*) That's how you talk to a father?
JAPHETH. (*Crosses to him.*) How should I talk?— Momma loves you dearly!

NOAH. Nobody loves me dearly. I would only be too damn tickled to death to see a proof!
JAPHETH. What would you call a proof?
NOAH. If you would remember to give God love an' respect!
JAPHETH. God doesn't want the respect of a slave upon its knees!
NOAH. You think you know what God wants? Take the rudder off! Because we didn't hit no house, sonny dear—we hit Leviathan, the whale! God sent him as a warning.
JAPHETH. We hit a house— I saw the roof!
NOAH. (*Exasperatedly.*) You foolish boy, you—if there can be such a thing as a whale, why can't he have a roof! Before it's too late I warn you—give up your brother's wife! Maybe this is the reason why Mother is sick . . . God sent a judgment against us . . . He'll take her away.
JAPHETH. (*Pausing.*) You don't believe that, do you . . . ?
NOAH. (*Slowly.*) You're right, I don't. Nothing will happen to Mother on the ark . . . (*Then, saddened and tender, the anger gone—sits bench* C.) Japhie, I would give my neck to have back your younger days—a boy like a picture you used to be! (*Gently.*) Once, in a dream last week, you cried in my arms . . .
JAPHETH. (*Sits* L. *of him. Softened.*) And once in a dream, long ago, you cried in my arms, Poppa . . .
NOAH. (*Tenderly.*) Japheth, couldn't you give up your wild ways? Listen to God's sweet voice . . .
JAPHETH. (*Bridling a little.*) But I think that's what I'm doing, Poppa.
NOAH. (*Tensing again.*) No, you're wrong . . .
JAPHETH. (*Tightening.*) I think I'm right . . .
NOAH. (*Rises. Blowing up again.*) Sonny, your ways is not good ways—the Lord will hang you by your tail!
JAPHETH. (*Rises.*) Poppa, dear, you'll have to accept me for what I am—not what you want me to be. (*Crosses* L.)
NOAH. I take pity on you. Finished! (*Crosses* R. *Shem enters* L. *and gives Japheth a drink.*)
SHEM. (*Crosses* R. *to Noah.*) Poppa, welcome home! What a relief to see you. How are you feeling?
NOAH. I'll live. . . .
SHEM. Poppa, I couldn't help thinking while you were gone, how when God picked you to head the ark, He picked an honest—in fact, a great man!

NOAH. What! I'm a loaf of bread. Don't butter me, Shem.

SHEM. And we owe Japheth a lot of credit, too.

NOAH. For what?

SHEM. Why, with his own hands last night, he saved the ark when it sprang a leak.

NOAH. Excuse me! God saved the ark!

SHEM. You see, Poppa, all I want to do is arbitrate here and . . .

NOAH. Second place, nothing is wrong with the ark!

JAPHETH. Nothing is wrong—?

SHEM. Excuse me, sir, until Japhie makes real repairs, the ark is leaking badly.

NOAH. And that, Sonny, is how it stays!

SHEM. (*Heart sinking.*) Whatta you mean? A sheep could walk through that hole!

NOAH. Make or break, it's how the Lord wants it. Only He can save the ark. It's punishment for your sins. (*Crosses* L. *to Japheth.*)

JAPHETH. You were drunk for nine weeks! Don't *you* ever get punished?

NOAH. (*Quickly.*) That's special . . . (*Crosses* R. *Then, spitting overboard.*) Sometimes God makes a little room for human nature . . .

JAPHETH. (*Angrily.*) But you don't and you never did—that's the trouble!

SHEM. (*Heartsick but trying.*) Poppa, I'm only a humble arbitrator here and—

NOAH. So arbitrate! This minute do God's work—Help me take the rudder off! (*Crosses* L.)

JAPHETH. (*Quickly.*) For the life of all we hold dear, don't touch that rudder!

SHEM. (*Pausing, in a low voice.*) Poppa . . . we'll have to defer to Japhie's knowledge . . . we're afloat in dangerous waters . . . I'm only trying to arbitrate. . . .

NOAH. (*Scornfully, walking away—crosses* R.) He found his self a new word, the fresh man—arbitrate! Can't help his self, but he wants to help God run the ark!

SHEM. (*Hurt.*) Excuse me, I know how to help myself!

NOAH. (*Angrily.*) Sure, you help yourself to any damn thing comes along!

SHEM. (*Helplessly but doggedly.*) Maybe my brain is clumsy

and unfit. I don't claim to be perfect—those days are over. But I'll still try to arbitrate between you and Japheth. Because you must learn to work together—the ark needs you both.
NOAH. (*The final insult.*) Outa town! Don't even hear you. (*Shem is stopped; his lips quiver and there are tears in his eyes.*)
SHEM. I guess I should shut up, just shut up . . . (*Sits bench* C.)
NOAH. That's right. When you have such little faith, you should keep you mouth shut!
JAPHETH. (*Voice quivering.*) How guilty you must feel for being drunk, to talk this way! (*Sits stern platform.*)
NOAH. Awright, enough talk. (*Crosses* L. *to door.*) I'll go down now an' see Mother.
SHEM. (*Face averted.*) And in my opinion, you underestimate how sick she is.
NOAH. (*Sadly.*) Here, also, you have no faith? Believe me on my life, nothing will happen to Mother on the ark . . . (*Ham enters quickly from the* R. *door.*)
HAM. Japheth, you'd better come right down!
SHEM. (*Nervously.*) What'sa matter . . . ?
HAM. (*Seeing Noah; crosses to Noah, insolently.*) Where were YOU?
NOAH. (*Dryly.*) Why, you missed me?
HAM. (*Coldly.*) I should shay sho!
SHEM. (*Swinging Ham around. Insistently.*) What'sa matter downstairs!
HAM. We're leaking bad again—the cows are in water up to the hocks!
SHEM. The plug pulled loose?
HAM. One corner tore right open! (*Hurrying out.*) I'm getting another mattress! (*Exits* R.)
SHEM. (*Calling after him.*) Get two more—we'll be right down! (*Nervously, to Japheth.*) I better get some extra candles—what else do you want?
NOAH. (*Between them.*) When you light the candles, look for the Lord's word on the wall.
SHEM. (*Agitatedly.*) Poppa, I'll ask you a big favor. Go down and stay with Momma.
JAPHETH. (*Crosses* C., *sits bench.*) Wait a minute, Shem. For months I've asked myself a question: is Poppa a saint or a fool?

Now I know he's half of each . . . but I never know which half is operating.

NOAH. (*Crosses D. L. Sharply.*) Shem, you'll tell a certain person I didn't hear his remarks!

SHEM. (*Growing wilder.*) Poppa, Japhie— GENTLEMEN!— there isn't time for all of this! (*Seeing Japheth sitting bench C.*) Why are you sitting there?

JAPHETH. What would YOU do right now?

SHEM. Plug up that leak!

JAPHETH. (*Standing restlessly.*) Poppa claims the ark is in Divine Hands only? Well, I'm ready to agree . . . we'll throw off the rudder. (*Crosses to Noah.*) And I'll give up Rachel and marry Goldie.

NOAH. Now at last the ark is in God's hands again, blessed be His Name! (*Crosses R.*)

SHEM. (*Crosses to L. door.*) Are you agreed on something? Now, let's all get down below.

JAPHETH. (*Crosses C. Sits bench. Quietly, unrushed.*) NO! Now there's no reason to go below.

SHEM. Have you lost your wits . . . ?

JAPHETH. No. I have faith, like Poppa. (*Noah is standing to one side, his hands clasped to his face in beatific gratitude. At this moment he is almost thrown to the deck by a single wallowing lurch of the ark.*)

SHEM. What was that?

JAPHETH. Water rushing into another hold.

SHEM. (*Despairingly.*) Do you hear that, Poppa? (*Noah is now looking down into the water and seems puzzled.*)

NOAH. Why is the water up so close . . . ? (*Japheth crosses L. to stern.*)

SHEM. (*Shouting.*) Don't you understand what's happening? Are you still drunk?

NOAH. (*Blinking his eyes.*) You're very excited, it looks to me . . .

SHEM. Are you asleep?

NOAH. You'll wake up everybody on the ark!

SHEM. Well, how do you want them to drown, asleep or awake?

NOAH. (*Very surprised.*) Whatta you mean drowned? (*Looking around a little.*) It's NOT stopping, Japhie?

JAPHETH. (*Calmly.*) I haven't bothered to look . . . (*Ham

rushes in R. *door and right out the* L., *lingering only long enough to say:*)

HAM. Get busy! Get mattresses! Cows are in water up to their udders!

NOAH. (*Crosses* C. *Shrinking somewhat.*) He said something? What did he say? He talked so fast.

SHEM. Poppa, (*Holding him.*) tell Japheth to go below!

NOAH. (*Pausing evasively.*) I should tell him . . . ? Why?

JAPHETH. (*Quietly.*) I'm ready, Poppa, to take the rudder off . . .

SHEM. Poppa, tell Japheth to go below and stopper up that hole!

JAPHETH. Poppa, I'm ready to take the rudder off right now!

NOAH. (*A little sickened but biding it.*) The rudder? *Now,* you mean? You wanna do it *now*?

SHEM. (*Still holding him by one arm.*) There is only a broken eggshell between us and the sea: the ark is sinking by inches! Tell Japheth to go to work with me!

NOAH. (*Slowly turning.*) Japhie, you think you should . . . ?

SHEM. Stop this insanity!

NOAH. Japhie knows about such things . . . he'll use his own judgment . . . (*Another lurch of the ark! The three men stagger. Cows' sounds, etc. Timidly.*) Sonny, why don't you use your judgment . . . you know, to fix . . .

JAPHETH. (*Simply.*) To use my own judgment, Poppa, I'd have to trust myself.

NOAH. (*Poignantly.*) So, really . . . *why* don't you trust yourself?

JAPHETH. Because you don't permit that!

NOAH. (*Crosses to Japheth. Meekly.*) But we can't do too much as God don't want it, can we?

JAPHETH. (*Pressing him.*) I don't know what you're talking about and I don't know what God wants, do you?

NOAH. (*Weakly.*) Do I what? (*Silence. The ark trembles a little.*)

SHEM. (*At the breaking point.*) Gentlemen—you two fanatics! —where do we go from here? (*Drained completely, Noah walks to the ark's edge and looks out, saying, with his back to the others:*)

NOAH. Japheth will go down with you, Shem . . .

JAPHETH. (*Crosses to Noah. Solemnly.*) No! No, I won't . . . not unless the rudder stays . . .

SHEM. You heard that, Poppa?
NOAH. (*In a very small voice.*) Awright, it stays.
JAPHETH. And you marry the four of us by noon today . . .
NOAH. Marry? (*With a wild turn.*) No, I'll never marry you! I'll drown in the water first. (*The ark wallows again. Noah sits bow. Shem pleads softly with Japheth, R. of him.*)
SHEM. Japheth, the fate of every living thing depends on you . . .
JAPHETH. (*To Shem or himself.*) I have a strange feeling that God changed today . . .
SHEM. (*Anxiously soft.*) Please . . . go down below!
JAPHETH. I'll go . . . but I never want to talk to Poppa again. (*He exits R. quickly. Shem, following him, stops to say a few quick words to Noah's little back:*)
SHEM. Go down and stay with Momma. And make no mistake she's very sick. Don't get in our way today. (*Then, voice trembling.*) I'm very ashamed to say it . . . but your youngest son is a better man of God than you! (*Shem hurries out. Noah alone, too hurt, too empty to move. [The few animals that have come up on deck a moment before are peering sadly at Noah.] Finally he says a few words, simply, desolately.*)
NOAH. The oldest day of my life . . . (*Then.*) What did I done, God . . . ? (*Sighing.*) I'll let the boys run things. I'll be the janitor on the ark . . . it fits to me. (*Picking up the gitka from the deck.*) Oh, gitka. My Esther is sick? Maybe dying? I'm ashamed to face her. God is far away, children . . . we're lonely people. (*He goes.*)

FADEOUT

CURTAIN

SCENE 8

Later, the ark by day.
On the deck there are two human beings and one other animal. Rachel is holding the tiller while Japheth is seated at her feet looking at the water. In the bow is sprawled the male lion, tired and muted, but looking yearningly

ahead. Noah's armchair has been placed C., L. *of the bench.*

RACHEL. (*Dreamily, after a pause.*) Hazy days, like autumn...
JAPHETH. (*Looking overboard.*) It's going somewhere very fast, that water—receding—and we're going right with it.
RACHEL. (*Happily.*) Our journey's almost over!
JAPHETH. (*Fondly, almost laughing.*) You're impatient—it may take weeks.
RACHEL. Then why did Poppa send out the two doves yesterday?
JAPHETH. He thinks they'll sight land—bring back a sign. It seems foolish to me.
RACHEL. Poppa seems so sad and alone—so old.
JAPHETH. Yeah, he's grown very old again the past few months, but no one tells him to be alone.
RACHEL. (*Softly.*) Talk to him, Japheth.
JAPHETH. (*Rises. Annoyed.*) I've tried many time, but he wants me to say I was wrong and I wasn't. He won't even talk to Momma!
RACHEL. That's silly! He's probably more worried than all of us put together.
JAPHETH. I don't believe it, Rachel. (*Then.*) Why that special look?
RACHEL. (*Rises—they embrace. Smiling.*) Because you're just like your father—love, wrath, gentleness and all. (*Noah enters from* R., *carrying a dove in a cage. Aware of their presence Noah stops. He is a sad, wistful and somewhat purged man, almost as old as he was before God transformed him; nevertheless there is a stubborn gleam in the heart of his new humility, and when he talks with his sons it will be only a formal matter, for connection he does not feel with them. Noah puts the cage on bench* C. *and deliberately coughs to announce that he is there. To Japheth.*) I'll go down and get you a snack. (*Sotto voce.*) Japheth, don't be stubborn...
NOAH. (*Sotto voce.*) Marry them? They'll wait an' whistle!... (*Rachel goes with a smile. Noah pretends to ignore Japheth and scans the skies with a sighing, worried air. Softly.*) Which little dove will find us land and return? (*Gloomily, to the Male Lion.*) Hello, Leon. They made you for a delegate to come up an' see what's happening? (*The Lion nodding.*) Don't be ashamed, brother

—it's your ark as well as it's mine . . . (*Then, with a sigh.*) You had trouble with your teeth, last week? . . . (*Sighing with commiseration.*) You're married *yourself* a long time? (*The Lion nodding.*) Yeh, it's a serious game. A wife, she'll make you sometimes to look like a two-cent piece, but it's still a wife. . . . (*Sadly, dropping his voice.*) my wife, she's not so active for a number of weeks awready. . . . She don't want me. . . . (*He lapses off with a sigh and the Lion joins him. Certain signs and colours in the sky begin to say the sun will be setting soon: there will be a beautiful, cooling twilight and a poignant afterglow. With a worried little flirt of a walk.*) I'll send out our last dove when it cools off.

JAPHETH. (*Calling politely.*) Why not band their feet, Poppa? Then you'd know which of the three came back.

NOAH. (*Stiffly.*) Then I'd know? Excuse me, I know them all by heart right now—Millie, Becky an' Judy here. (*Shem enters through the L. door, picking his teeth. Noah turns away without a word as Shem goes to the rudder.*)

SHEM. How're we doing up here? How's the pull on the rudder?

JAPHETH. Very strong but steady—we're picking up speed, too. I won't like it when it gets dark.

SHEM. (*Looking and considering.*) Hmmm . . . want me to spell you?

JAPHETH. Later.

SHEM. (*Turning.*) What're you doing there, Poppa? Hiding? (*Goldie enters L. Crosses U. L. behind housing.*)

NOAH. Don't worry. I won't get in your way today. (*Which is what he has begun to do with a little broom. Meanwhile Goldie comes out through the L. door and takes a basin of peelings to the other side of the ark and dumps them. Shem turns back to Japheth, dropping his voice.*)

SHEM. What's stirred him up again?

JAPHETH. He's anxious about his doves . . . that's all he thinks about.

SHEM. (*Sotto voce.*) I wish he'd get more anxious about Momma. By the way, she wants me to thank you for the eggs.

JAPHETH. What eggs?

SHEM. Those fresh eggs you sneak in and leave her every morning.

JAPHETH. I don't leave her any eggs. (*Shem turns and looks at*

Noah who sheepishly ducks behind the housing. Goldie crosses D. R. *from behind housing.*)
SHEM. I can't make him out, can you? (*Shem and Japheth listen to Goldie, who, about to go below, stops for a brief chat with Noah.*)
GOLDIE. Hello, Poppa. I love to call you Poppa.
NOAH. How is the gitka, Girlie? You're seein' her every day?
GOLDIE. Yes, she's fine—she stays right with Momma.
NOAH. Yeh, I know. And Mother, how is she?
GOLDIE. She looks better today, but we all wish you'd come down and see her.
NOAH. (*Evasively.*) I'm watchin' out for the doves. (*Goldie smiles at Noah and goes. Shem crosses to Noah.*)
SHEM. I can watch for a dove, too, Poppa. Why don't you go down and spend an hour with Momma? She keeps asking for you.
NOAH. I see her when she's sleepin' sometimes, don't I? Now let me alone, the bunch of you. I'm watchin' for the doves. (*Crosses* U. R. *Shem sits* C.)
JAPHETH. What are you fighting about? You and your doves!
NOAH. (*Crosses to Shem. Haughtily and quietly.*) Tell a certain person Mother will feel better on the ground. That's why I'm watchin' for the doves. I'm tryin' to find her a little piece of land soon in the worst way.
JAPHETH. What do you mean? You're afraid that Momma will die?
NOAH. No! Yes, I am afraid! I cannot see any future without Mother! If she dies, I will go right with her . . . so help me, God, which is true.
SHEM. (*Rises.*) If you're afraid, Poppa, let's be afraid together.
NOAH. (*Shaking his head.*) No, Sonny, that's no medicine to me. (*He goes up behind the housing. Rachel enters* L. *and goes to Japheth giving him a handful of figs. Ham enters* R. *and crosses down to Shem.*)
HAM. Nothing new with the doves?
SHEM. No. (*Goldie enters* R. *Sits in bow.*)
HAM. Are we sending out the other one?
SHEM. It's up to Poppa.
RACHEL. I'm sick to see something green. (*Ham crosses to Goldie in the bow.*)
HAM. I have news for you, Snake, I love you.

GOLDIE. (*Lovingly.*) By the way, I hate you.
NOAH. (*Coming down* L. *from behind housing. To Rachel.*) Tuchter, watch out for a dove. You got sharp eyes from your needlework.
RACHEL. Yes, I will, Poppa. (*She crosses up* L. *Noah crosses* R.)
SHEM. I have a hunch we won't get any sleep tonight. (*Just as Noah is about to pick up the cage, Esther appears in the* L. *door, she is breathing heavily and is assisted by Leah from behind. Rachel crosses to them.*)
ESTHER. (*Heavily.*) Uhh! Can't go up an' down the damn steps no more . . . that's right, Goldie, take the hat . . . (*Rachel has removed the hat from the chair and Esther sits heavily, the girls fussily making her comfortable. She is suffering from a wasting disease and her appearance is shocking. Noah takes one quick look at her and disappears around the housing. Goldie crosses to them.*) It's miserable hot downstairs. The flies could eat you up alive. (*To Rachel.*) Now I'll take the hat, honey . . .
RACHEL. You look fine, Momma . . .
ESTHER. (*Stolidly.*) I look like hell, not fine. Go, Goldie, take care—finish the supper. I'll take the gitka. Goldie's learning—she'll make a very tasty supper. (*Goldie puts the gitka in Esther's lap and goes below with a smile—*R. *Esther has put on the large flora-laden hat and Ham admires it from the bow.*)
HAM. You look like a queen, Momma! . . .
ESTHER. (*Settled and looking around.*) Where's Poppa? Noah . . . ? He hiding again? (*Calling angrily.*) Noah! (*Noah timidly and innocently appears around the housing with the broom in his hand*)
NOAH. (*Crosses* D. R. *Meekly.*) You want me, Esther? I'm sweepin'. . . .
ESTHER. Go, children, I wanna be with my husband alone.
NOAH. (*Defiantly, to Shem.*) Esther, you came up for fresh air. (*Esther looks at him scornfully as the children discreetly scatter, Shem joining Japheth for a whispered conference at the rudder.*)
ESTHER. If you would look how you look, it's only a shame . . .
NOAH. (*Falteringly.*) Maybe I'll get you something, a few crackers, a muffin—?
ESTHER. (*Annoyed.*) Noah, I'll bite your ears off in a minute! You couldn't come down to see me? Put the broom away, you fool!
NOAH. (*Growing huffy.*) Now, now, my dear lady—it's not

necessary, such a talk. (*Abruptly, seeing her wince.*) How are you feelin'?
ESTHER. Don't dance an' put the broom away. (*Sarcastically.*) Otherwise I'm afraid you'll hit me. (*Beckoning.*) Come closer.
NOAH. Me? (*Crosses to her.*)
ESTHER. Come closer . . . (*Waiting until he does. Noah sits on bench—close to her.*) Marry the children . . . for the sake of happiness in the world . . .
NOAH. Old friend, it hurts me to refuse you, but it stands in the books for a thousand years—
ESTHER. (*Head nodding.*) But all the books in the water now . . . marry the children before I go . . .
NOAH. (*Scoffingly.*) That's foolish, Tuchter! First place, he won't permit such marriages, the God I know. And secondly, He won't let nothing happen to you, the God I know.
ESTHER. (*Growing very tired.*) Maybe you don't know Him . . . any more . . .
NOAH. (*Cheering her up.*) Don't you worry, we'll have a promised land together. I'm your particular friend, hear me?
ESTHER. (*Shaking her head weakly.*) The children, their happiness . . . is my last promised land. . . .
NOAH. (*Worried.*) You're tired?
ESTHER. (*Absently.*) The gitka didn't sing a long time . . .
NOAH. No, you can't make her if she don't wanna. . . . (*Ham calls abruptly from the bow, where he has just been joined by Goldie.*)
HAM. Aren't we picking up speed?
JAPHETH. (*Making another sounding.*) Yes.
SHEM. (*Calling.*) We won't get much sleep tonight with this speed we're picking up. And it's getting dark, too!
NOAH. (*Looking around alertly.*) Dark? How will a dove find us in the dark?
LEAH. (*Sitting on the bench.*) There's a moon tonight.
RACHEL. I'm watching, Poppa.
NOAH. Good girl . . .
ESTHER. But the sun's over there now, not here. . . .
NOAH. Ham! Ham! Help Momma—
JAPHETH. (*Hovering nearby.*) Ham, help me move Mamma . . . around in the sun . . . (*Ham promptly joining Japheth. In carry-*

ing Esther in her chair around the house into the remaining patch of sunlight.)

ESTHER. I'll take the hat to shade my eyes. (*Dizzily.*) Help me . . . I'm a baby, I'm a baby . . . Noah, I'll tell you a mystery— (*Noah stands, at a loss, uneasy, again looking at the sky and generally around the ark.*)

NOAH. We're the only living people in the world and Esther is down and out. I'll put a great big page on the table an' I'll write it out some day, what happened on this trip . . . it's a lonely story, God. What was it for?

SHEM. The rudder's getting teasier and crankier by the minute! (*Noah turns to the sons at the rudder and at this moment Rachel calls out with excitement:*)

RACHEL. Poppa, I think that's a bird!

NOAH. Where? (*Everyone except Shem and the bewildered Lion moves down the deck to where Rachel is standing and pointing. Noah shades his eyes with his hand.*) She's white . . . ?

RACHEL. Is it the dove?

JAPHETH. It's one of the doves!

SHEM. It's her, all right!

HAM. What's she circling like that for?

LEAH. Maybe she didn't see us.

SHEM. Yeah, maybe she don't see us.

RACHEL. She's turning!

NOAH. Which one is it? Come in, Tuchter—I'm here—come in my arms! I'll bless you in all the years to come!

JAPHETH. She's tired.

SHEM. Yeah . . .

NOAH. (*Fervidly.*) When I go down in my casket I'll remember her!

HAM. Here she comes!

NOAH. It's Millie . . . ?

SHEM. Here she comes! (*There is a swift fluttering almost unseen swoop and the dove plunges into the knot of humans.*)

NOAH. Careful! I got her—it's Becky! (*Crying.*) How it beats, how it beats—her whole body is a heart!

GOLDIE. What's in her mouth? (*The group has opened a little. Noah takes a small green leaf from the bird's mouth and hands the bird to Japheth.*)

NOAH. Look! Look! A green leaf, from an olive tree! There is land somewhere!
RACHEL. A leaf!
SHEM. (*Awed.*) Oh, God in heaven!
GOLDIE. A green leaf. . . .
NOAH. A tree! Esther, there is open land in the world somewhere! Our trip is done, old friend, and— (*He has turned and is starting for Esther. This is followed by the falsetto voice of the gitka singing an undeniable mourning song, which tells Noah that something dreadful is taking place behind the housing.*) Go . . . Shem . . . see what Momma . . . she . . . (*Shem crosses* U. L. *behind housing, returns with Esther's hat, crosses* D. C. *to Noah.*)
SHEM. Her hat fell off. She's dead, Poppa.
NOAH. I'll sit . . . no, I'll go stand by the wall. (*Shouting.*) What?! You'll go so far but don't you go too far! What?! You'll all make me so mad I'll eat you up to pieces! (*Motionless.*) Shem, tell me the truth, make or break—
SHEM. She's dead.
NOAH. (*With an abrupt howl.*) Jaaphieee! I have trouble. Sonny, help me. I'm in trouble. (*He puts himself in Japheth's arms and cries like a child. Recovered, he wipes his eyes and says:*) Children, the whole night is ahead to give thanks to Heaven. Go better now every husband should kiss each wife, as Mother wanted. And I'll go kiss mine and close her eyes . . . (*He goes around the housing* U. L.)

CURTAIN

SCENE 9

TIME: *Later.*
PLACE: *Adjacent to the ark aground.*
We are looking at a Japanese print by Hiroshege. The ark has come to earth in a very high place, surrounded by lucent early morning sky on all sides. The craft is gently tipped to one side, deep in what was mud but now is dry soil. A centrally-placed gangplank leads down to a strip of Gauguin-pink earth in front. At L. *a young peach tree grows in profuse and handsome bloom.*

Rachel, at L. of the gangplank, rests against a small heap of bundles and luggage. Goldie does likewise at R., her heart is in the highlands. Ham, above her on the deck, lounges lazily, improvising humorous remarks for her ears alone; She giggles and laughs, but thinks she should be feeling solemn.

Shem and Leah are still busy with their belongings. Leah, like the other women, is very swollen with child, but she is helping her husband add to an enormous stack of bundles heaped up at far R.; husband and wife are very serious and singleminded about their work.

Noah and Japheth are missing. From below the hill comes the occasional lowering of cattle; from behind comes the keen song or musical points of this bird and that. But above all, if unheard by the personages of the play, sounds the shimmering hum of the presence of God; Noah, one should judge, is somewhere in a conference.

GOLDIE. (*Giggling.*) He keeps making me laugh . . . now stop it, Ham! (*But instead Ham makes her laugh again with another whispered sally. Shem glances at them both with annoyance.*)
SHEM. (*Impatiently.*) I wish Poppa would hurry. I wanna start before the sun gets higher.
HAM. Shem, let history record that one year ago you came aboard with eight bundles—you're leaving with twenty-nine! Why did Poppa give you the two extra cows?
SHEM. Because I'm a responsible citizen, will ya!
LEAH. (*Loftily.*) And Poppa will probably come to live with us.
HAM. No, I think he'll go with Japheth. Won't he, Rachel?
RACHEL. (*Quietly.*) Why not wait and see . . . (*Everything has come to rest by now. Leah sitting as Shem adds the last bundle to his stack. Only the sounds of nature are heard for a moment.*)
GOLDIE. Maybe Poppa'll go with us. I can cook all his favorite dishes—Momma taught me. (*Japheth comes up from below and goes to Rachel and stares solemnly at the little peach tree.*)
SHEM. Is he coming up yet?
JAPHETH. His door is still closed.
GOLDIE. (*To herself.*) I love to call him Poppa . . .
RACHEL. (*Looking out.*) The world looks washed . . . (*Here*

he is, old Noah, humorous, gentle and affable, very affectionate with here and there a lost, wistful touch, there is nowhere a trace of his old impatient and authoritarian attitudes. He is wearing a strange little hat on the back of his head, his arms are filled with Esther's one-leafed plant and Becky, the dove in a wicker cage.)

HAM. Here's Poppa!

NOAH. All the animals went away? Nothing at all's left on board?

JAPHETH. No, sir.

LEAH. *(Abruptly.)* We'd all like to know what you decided, Poppa. Who'll you go with?

GOLDIE. Yes, we're all waiting to know, Poppa.

NOAH. Children—I'll stay with Shem. Why? It's more comfortable.

GOLDIE. Poppa, Poppa—how I'll miss you!

NOAH. Go now, children, an' be fruitful and multiply . . . an' everywhere and in all things, replenish the earth—

SHEM. Let's start, Poppa, before the sun gets too high.

NOAH. Go ahead. I'll catch up.

HAM. *(Crosses to Rachel.)* Rachel, will you think of me sometimes?

RACHEL. Yes. Every time I have a toothache.

HAM. *(Laughingly to Japheth.)* You're a strange bird, son. *(Crosses R.)*

JAPHETH. *(Grinning.)* You're a strange duck, Ham. *(Ham hoists his bundles and calls over:)*

HAM. See you down the hill, Poppa. *(Meanwhile Goldie and Rachel have kissed and embraced, the former doing the same with Japheth as she says:)*

GOLDIE. You can't get very close to me, can you?

LEAH. Goodbye, Rachael.

SHEM. *(Calling.)* Rachel, keep well.

RACHEL. *(Calling.)* Be happy, Shem.

LEAH. *(To all.)* I hope everyone gets everything their hearts desire. *(There are more smiles and chatter and as they start off right with arms loaded Goldie calls back in departure:)*

GOLDIE. We'll wait down below to say goodbye, Poppa.

NOAH. *(Waving.)* Yeh, yeh . . . be careful, girls, going down the hill. Boys, hold the girls. . . . *(They go off noisily. Shem, having waited silently, gives Japheth a clumsy and tight bearhug,*

wordlessly he goes to his bundles slinging them into practical units and exits R. *Japheth is meanwhile looking out at the land below. A hush falls over the scene. Noah, from above.*) What kinda tree is so beautiful?
JAPHETH. It's a flowering peach, Poppa.
NOAH. Peach. . . . (*Thinking a long thought.*) Before you look up . . . it's the first April without Mother. (*Japheth has broken off a small branch of the bloom and hands it to Rachel who turns and gives it to Noah. This precious gift he accepts with a nuance of smile and exquisite care, murmuring:*) From the new earth.
RACHEL. Now we are a story—a legend.
JAPHETH. What's ahead, Poppa?
NOAH. (*Holding up the bloom.*) This is ahead . . . a fruitful world . . . the people need happiness. For a year we stood in a boat an' looked ourself in the face.
JAPHETH. We were forced to face ourself, you mean?
NOAH. I'm listening, tell me. . . .
JAPHETH. I don't know. But we've all changed.
NOAH. An' He changed, too . . . ?
JAPHETH. Maybe God changes when men change.
NOAH. (*Sighing.*) An' now you'll leave me, children . . . ?
JAPHETH. Yes, sir. (*Noah embraces Rachel tenderly, saying:*)
NOAH. I pray a beautiful soul shall enter your baby. . . .
RACHEL. Goodbye, Poppa . . .
JAPHETH. Goodbye, Poppa dear. Poppa—thank you.
NOAH. Careful, Tuchter.
RACHEL. Goodbye, ark. . . .
NOAH. (*Mutely.*) Write sometimes. . . .
RACHEL. (*Eyes wet.*) Yes. . . . (*They exit* L., *Rachel one time looking back longingly. Noah is waving a little forlorn hand at them long after they disappeared. Then he wipes his nose with the back of a hand, sniffing and looking around at the ark:*)
NOAH. Right here I could sleep out my remaining years . . . till my Esther wants me. . . . (*Then he cocks his head with a bemused smile, for like us he hears the returning Presence of God. Dreamily.*) You're hanging around, Lord? That's just how I feel. (*Listening.*) No, I won't get off the ark. Forgive me, Sir, excuse me . . . first a little guarantee, a covenant, an' then I'll go. . . . (*Watchful and waiting.*) You know what I want, Lord. Just like You guarantee each month, with a woman's blood, that

men will be born . . . give such a sign that you won't destroy the world again. . . . (*He waits tensely until the music hum relaxes into a quality of benevolence, and relaxing and smiling, asks:*) Where shall I look? Where? (*Anyone who would be watching sees the rainbow in the sky before Noah turns and sees it with an awed clasping of his hands. With awed happiness.*) Thank you, Lord above, thank you. . . . (*Abruptly cocking his head.*) But what I learned on the trip, dear God, you can't take it away from me. To walk in humility, I learned. (*Crosses to* D. *ramp.*) And listen, even to *myself* . . . and to speak softly, with the voices of consolation. Yes, I hear You, God—now it's in man's hands to make or destroy the world.— I'll tell you a mystery. . . .

CURTAIN

PROPERTY PLOT

Scene 1—Home:

Table—jug of water, cup of water
2 benches
1 chair
Stool
Cupboard—brandy, bread, various utensils, cups, pottery
Water jug
Brandy jug (or bottles)
Bread
Various utensils
Tablecloth—off L.
Candlesticks—off R.

Scene 2—Home:

Knife (for Japheth)—carries, also his shoes—D. L.
Wooden spoon (partially made)
Wooden spoon (for Leah)
Table setting for seven—plates, cups, spoons, etc.—off L.
Sabbath bread
Brandy
Candlesticks—off L.
Lighted sliver of wood—off L.
Gitka (on Noah)
Seedless raisins in cupboard and on table for Shem

Scene 3—High Hillside:

Flowers—plants
Table
Vats, crocks, baskets—around table
Olives, dates, figs, cheese, bread, several cucumbers—paring knife
Wrappings for food (leaves)
4 water buckets
Milk pail
Bunch of keys on chain (Leah)
Long half-peeled log
Leaf fan—bench D. L.

Water pitcher
Stick (for Japheth)
Cups, plates—on table—opening
3 stools
Lemons, figs and dates on table
Milk bucket on floor with Rachel
By rock: water buckets—U. C. (6)
Cucumbers—off L.
Gitka on stage in box—on rock—Scenes III, IV, V
Dipper by spring: opening
Cups by spring: opening

Scene 4—High Hillside:

Shelter (canopy on rustic sticks)
Carrots (in container)

On table:
　Paring knife
　Lemons
　Dates
　Figs
　Packet of figs
Grass
Sewing (for Rachel)
Staff (for Noah)
Stick: club—R. rock

On table:
　Cups
　Water
Pitcher
2 bags of seeds (Noah)—off L.
Fans
Keys
4 water tumblers
Various bundles, crates, etc.
Dish of potatoes on table (Leah)
Dipper by spring
Keys (worn by Leah)

Scene 5—High Hillside:

Loom—holding partially woven piece of cloth
Woolen cloth

Various foodstuffs and household articles—by bench
Bags of grain and animal food—off U. L.—also, all around rocks
Hay
Luggage (for Japheth) 2 bundles—off L.
Large hat (Esther—has hat when curtain goes up)
Crust of bread (for Noah)
Sawdust box (for Gitka)
Baskets
Olive oil jars
Fans, electric—for wind
Leaves to blow
Thunder screen

Scene 6—The Ark:

Tools—mallet and chisel (for Japheth)—tool kit and apron
Gitka (on Noah)
Damp clothes—various colors, hanging—including sheets
Fish line
Slop buckets (2)—in ark house—R.
Small rubber plant—in ark house—R.
Palm leaf fans

Scene 7—The Ark:

Tiller, loop ropes for tiller
Lamps—put in cabin
Gitka (in Noah's pocket)

Scene 8—The Ark:

Figs
Sounding line—on stage above rudder
Broom—Ham using at opening at bow
Tape and padding—by rudder in opening
Vegetable refuse, in pan or bucket—in cabin
Wicker bird cage—in cabin
Armchair—on in opening
Rubber plant (only two leaves—one yellowed and dying) in cabin
Large basket (Leah)—in cabin
Olive pits (and containers)—in cabin in basket
Hat (Esther) on armchair in opening
Palm leaf fan (Esther)
Pail of water—by rudder

Dove (pocket of Noah)
Green leaf, olive (pocket of Noah)
Gitka—in cabin

Scene 9—On Shore:

Bundles and luggage
Peach tree
Dove, in cage
Plant

New TITLES

A WALK IN THE WOODS
BURN THIS
THE BOYS NEXT DOOR
GUS AND AL
HEATHEN VALLEY
AMERICAN NOTES
EVENING STAR
SHOOTING STARS
MAX AND MAXIE
YEAR OF THE DUCK
THE JOHNSTOWN VINDICATOR
A GRAND ROMANCE
ONE THING MORE
THE ROAD TO THE GRAVEYARD
CROSSIN' THE LINE

● *Write for Information*

DRAMATISTS PLAY SERVICE, INC.
440 Park Avenue South   New York, N. Y. 10016

New  PLAYS

FRANKIE AND JOHNNY IN THE CLAIR DE LUNE

LAUGHING WILD

ANOTHER ANTIGONE

THE RED DEVIL BATTERY SIGN

NORTH SHORE FISH

THE WEDDING OF THE SIAMESE TWINS

HEART OF A DOG

BURKIE

THE VAMPYRE

ANOTHER SEASON'S PROMISE

CANDY & SHELLEY GO TO THE DESERT

VALENTINE'S DAY

PLANET FIRES

DOG LADY & THE CUBAN SWIMMER

INQUIRIES INVITED

 DRAMATISTS PLAY SERVICE, INC.
440 Park Avenue South　　New York, N.Y. 10016

New PLAYS

EASTERN STANDARD
BORDERLINES
AMULETS AGAINST THE DRAGON FORCES
THE MAGIC ACT
KILLERS
THE DEATH OF PAPA
IMPASSIONED EMBRACES
CLEVER DICK
LOVE MINUS
BIG MARY
FAITH, HOPE & CHARITY
ELECTION YEAR & SO WHEN WE GET MARRIED
TWO EGGS SCRAMBLED SOFT & A BRIEF PERIOD OF TIME

DRAMATISTS PLAY SERVICE, INC.
440 Park Avenue South   New York, N.Y. 10016

RECENT

Releases . . .

THE COCKTAIL HOUR
BRILLIANT TRACES
HENRY LUMPER
PLAYERS IN A GAME
WOMAN AND WATER
SLEEPING DOGS
THE DAY ROOM
COUSINS
DEMON WINE
THE TRICKERIES OF SCAPIN
THEN AND NOW
REBEL ARMIES DEEP INTO CHAD
WAITING FOR LEFTY
JULIET, YANCEY, APRIL SNOW
ROOMMATES

Write for information as to availability

DRAMATISTS PLAY SERVICE, Inc.
440 Park Avenue South   New York, N.Y. 10016

New PLAYS

**THE HEIDI CHRONICLES
ITALIAN AMERICAN RECONCILIATION
LOVE LETTERS
ZERO POSITIVE
CASH FLOW
SAVED FROM OBSCURITY
DEEP SLEEPERS
DALTON'S BACK
PLAYING WITH FIRE (after Frankenstein)
RIGHT BEHIND THE FLAG
ABSTINENCE
WOMEN AND WALLACE
THE MAN WHO CLIMBED THE PECAN TREES**

Inquiries Invited

DRAMATISTS PLAY SERVICE, INC.
440 Park Avenue South   New York, N. Y. 10016

NEW PLAYS

APOCALYPTIC BUTTERFLIES
ANCIENT HISTORY
BEEN TAKEN
A FLEA IN HER EAR
THE HEART OUTRIGHT
FOG ON THE MOUNTAIN
MR. WILLIAMS AND MISS WOOD
OATMEAL AND KISSES
PVT. WARS (Full Length)
TO CULEBRA
REASONABLE CIRCULATION
ASCENSION DAY
THE DOCTOR WILL SEE YOU, NOW
THE LAST GOOD MOMENT OF LILY BAKER

Write for information as to availability

DRAMATISTS PLAY SERVICE, Inc.
440 Park Avenue South   New York, N.Y. 10016

NEW PLAYS

CARNAL KNOWLEDGE
THE LOMAN FAMILY PICNIC
THE MOONSHOT TAPE
A POSTER OF THE COSMOS
THE MODEL APARTMENT
AMATEURS
CARBONDALE DREAMS
SALLY BLANE, WORLD'S GREATEST GIRL DETECTIVE
MOON OVER THE BREWERY
THE MEETING
THE STONEWATER RAPTURE
THE SHOW MUST GO ON
SEEING SOMEONE
IF WALLS COULD TALK

Write for information as to availability
DRAMATISTS PLAY SERVICE, Inc.
440 Park Avenue South   New York, N.Y. 10016